Rookie Dad

Rookie Dad

adventures in Fatherhood

by Rick Epstein

HYPERION
New York

Library of Congress Cataloging-in-Publication Data

Epstein, Rick
  Rookie dad : adventures in fatherhood / by Rick Epstein.—1st ed.
    p. cm.
  ISBN 1–56282–970–X : $16.95 ($21.95 Can.)
  1. Fatherhood—United States. 2. Fathers and daughters—United States. I. Title.
HQ756.E67 1992
306.874'2—dc20   92–1106
                                                            CIP

                              FIRST EDITION

                    10 9 8 7 6 5 4 3 2 1

For Betsy

Although a few names have been changed,
this is a work of nonfiction
and any resemblance
to real persons and events
is just too bad.

Introduction

The surgeon whipped a purple baby out of a hasty incision and presto! I was a father. I'd been warned months ago it would happen but when it did, fatherhood seemed to occur suddenly. One minute I was an apprehensive husband trying to get up the courage to peek around the green cotton draperies on my wife's thorax and the next minute I was an overwhelmed father with tears of emotion rolling down my pale face.

The surgeon handed the baby off to the pediatrician who took it aside and did some brisk, routine things to it, put a little hat on its head, and placed the baby into my arms. I glanced back at my unconscious wife who lay on the operating table as nurses and doctors decided which of the tissues and organs had to go back in and which should be discarded. With any kind of luck Betsy would be okay —that's what I would have told myself if I hadn't been so absorbed in the bundle I was cradling in my arms.

With a doctor leading the way, I walked slowly and carefully toward the nursery like someone carrying a saucer of nitroglycerine through a crowd of practical jokers. But no one slapped me on the back or extended a leg to trip me. In the corridor the baby's eyes opened for the first time. They were murky and dark and as unfocused as postholes. To me, however, those eyes seemed to be drinking me in, getting a first impression. I regretted the silly-looking, blue shower-cap thing they'd made me put on in the OR.

After a half hour of sitting in the nursery just holding the baby and admiring it (I wouldn't really think of the baby as female for another year or so), a nurse told me Betsy would sleep for another couple of hours. So I surrendered the child and went home to shower and change clothes for work.

Walking out into the lot I found the car I'd parked so hastily the night before. Had it been only the night before? I half-expected to find its tires flat, battery dead and lichen growing on its windows as if it had been left moldering for years. I was surprised to find the ignition key in my pocket and such surprises continued for a few days until my world settled down into a decreasingly wobbly new orbit.

After those vivid and memorable first moments came a year that was numbing and unpleasant for me. So I don't have much information on it. Sure, there's a baby book in which Betsy wrote the important firsts with regard to such feats as rolling over and eating cereal. And there are albums full of photos of a moon-headed baby variously sleeping, eating, crying, smiling, bathing, and just lying there. But my own memory yields little about Baby Marie. I seem to recall changing a lot of diapers, waking up at night to bring her to Betsy for milking, and pacing the nursery floor holding a squalling infant against my shoulder. Betsy seems to remember me leaving the house frequently.

My own diaries, recognized by family and friends as a fairly complete and reliable source of hard fact, historical color, and light philosophy, likewise shed very little light on that first year. In June, when Marie would have been six months old, there was a mention of a "drooling, incontinent little troll" but it may have been a reference to a co-worker.

To tell the truth, Marie didn't really captivate me until she started talking and toddling. Then the fascination was so acute, that I had to sort it out and write it down.

Part 1

Marie

1. Connecticut

It was a difficult time, that weekend in Connecticut. It was one of those visits during which new parents notice that a chasm has opened to separate them from childless friends.

Four of us—all 1969 graduates of Lawrence High School in New Jersey—had remained close and one of our number, Doug, was hosting us, plus wives, at a place he was renting from Theodore Roosevelt's granddaughter in a fancy rural neighborhood.

I sat on the floor of an old but solid playhouse observing with adoration my eighteen-month-old daughter, who was bustling clumsily around with the few props the years had overlooked—a little table and chair and a toy broom. I generally observe Marie with adoration, but this day there was a tinge of desperation to it. I was determined not to resent her for keeping me from my pals, who were about two hundred feet away, through some woods, in the big house, probably drinking beer and talking about politics, movies, or memorable girls of LHS.

Since then, my wife Betsy and I have learned to bring coloring books, storybooks, videotapes, and other amusement equipment when we go visiting. But we were pretty green then and like an ill-supplied army, we had to forage. Doug's old house was barren terrain. It was almost as if General Sherman had led a marrauding army of tots through the place and they'd burned or carried off anything that would entertain Marie.

We found one old children's book—*Little Black Sambo*. The title was jarring and I hated to benefit from the British colonialism that spawned this tale of India, but the story itself was charming. So whenever it was my turn to mind Marie, we'd sit in an armchair and take Sambo through his travails and then Marie would say, "Tiny house," and off we'd toddle through the woods to kill some time there.

On the second day word filtered through the forest to me that we were all about to pile into two cars and go check out the South Norwalk Street Fair. Submissive family man that I am, I rode with Marie and the wives. Once the boys got a look at the fair, they decided they could do better and, before I could negotiate my release, they'd driven off without me.

For the rest of the long afternoon Betsy and I took turns pushing the stroller and amusing Marie and looking at handcrafted broom covers and other items equally compelling.

For Marie, the memorable part of the day came when she was toddling around with a helium balloon tied to her wrist. A heedless teenage boy rushing past got between her and the balloon, running afoul of the string. This knocked her off her pudgy pins onto the pavement. She wasn't really hurt, but for weeks she'd be telling anyone who'd listen, "Boy knock me down."

The final day saw Marie and me back on the Sambo/tiny-house circuit. I considered bringing the book into the playhouse for a read there, but that kind of efficiency would have been counterproductive. Instead I passed the time in that outpost admiring my child at play and interacting only enough to keep her busy. An idea came to me, and I said, "Marie, when we get home, I'm going to build you a tiny house."

She didn't understand, but I became consumed with the idea.

My brief time as a father had turned me into a philosopher—not a very smart or original one, I suppose, but I had begun thinking when I normally would've had the radio on. And the main fruit of all this dead air was the thought that a good childhood is the one, big, everlasting gift that parents give a child. And everything, from the quality of grass in the yard to what you tell a child about death, is an element of that gift.

It struck me that day that a well-built playhouse in the backyard would be just the kind of hands-on, stage-prop, imagination-firing monument to paternal love that would upgrade Marie's childhood like aluminum siding on a two-bedroom Cape Cod.

I took my notebook and pen out of my pocket and started sketching details of construction of the playhouse. Pacing off measurements and drawing intersections of wall and roof, I gave Marie only perfunctory responses.

But when we returned to our own home back in New Jersey, I was greeted by my half-finished fence— a poorly conceived project that mutely demanded that I finish it before starting on the next one.

2. The safety fence

When I was about ten, a Little Leaguer out in the Midwest was killed by a pitched baseball, a tragedy that sent shock waves back to our house in New Jersey. My mom told my big brother and me that if we still wanted to play ball, we'd have to use a softball in our after-school sandlot games.

But softball was for girls and old men, and we played ball with the regular kind of preteen, punch-you-on-the-arm boys who believed it was effeminate to call a guy by his first name. I tried to picture myself saying to them, "Hey guys, let's use a softball today; my mom's afraid a hardball might kill us." No way. I could just as easily have said, "Baseball again? Why don't we put on some of our moms' old dresses and play Beauty Parlor?"

The best solution would have been to come up with a pair of those hard-plastic batting helmets they have nowadays, but I don't think they'd been invented by 1961. At least they hadn't trickled down to us. But we did have a couple of steel, World War II, Army surplus helmet liners that Dad had given us for Christmas. Mom agreed to let us play hardball if we wore those helmets.

So we got to play baseball and protect our manliness at the same time though we were a strange sight the rest of the season. Besides being safe from beanballs and red-hot line drives, we would've stood a decent chance against sniper fire and shrapnel.

Had my mom overreacted? I thought so until Marie's birth suddenly endowed me with the gruesome imagination of a Stephen King.

It has eased a little with time, but in those first couple of years my mind was constantly playing out horrible worst-case scenarios. In them, the usual laws of gravity and inertia and behavior gave way to new forces and motivations that had my baby embracing a red-hot woodstove and sent pointed objects of all sorts toward those dear little eyes that everyone says look so much like mine. Tripping over nothing, she'd break her tiny white teeth on hard sidewalks, or our disinterested cat would, without motivation, sink unfriendly claws into tender flesh. I had dreams, too. In the worst of them Marie was cooked by hoboes.

I asked Betsy if she had these visions of calamity and disfigurement and she said yes, but only a little. The fact is, Betsy doesn't need premonitions.

She has the reflexes of a shortstop. While I'm musing, "Gee, isn't the baby getting a little close to the edge of the chair?" Betsy is sweeping in for a shoestring catch before Junior hits the floor. Can all mothers think with their spinal cords, or just the major-leaguers?

So instead of reflexes, I have paranoia. In the springtime, when Marie was just beginning to toddle, she celebrated her first moment of outdoor mobility in the frontyard by running out into the street. There are no sidewalks in our neighborhood and the front walk extends sixteen feet from our front steps and terminates in the street. An invitation to tragedy.

True, ours is the last house on a dead-end street so there is no traffic. But what if someone didn't know it was a dead-end street? And what if just at that moment Marie went rocketing down the front walk? And what if the driver didn't see her? Or what if his brakes were defective?

A fence was needed and I would build it. I have never been much of a woodworker. At Lawrence Junior High School I never finished a shop project, though I blame the teacher for that. When I would approach Mr. Donald for advice, he'd look at the abused bits of lumber in my hands the way Dracula looks at a crucifix. Wordlessly, he'd shake his head with dismay and loathing and back away. As far as I know, his supply closet still contains my unfinished bird-feeder and most of a letter-rack.

But Marie's dash into the street had emboldened me to try again. The next day I was in the Hunterdon County Library's how-to section looking up fences. Most of them seemed too flimsy, so I designed my own. A couple of months later I had the front edge of the yard barricaded by a mighty wooden fence and gate, so overdone that my hypothetical motorist could drive straight at it and still not get to our stoop.

Most important, though, there was no way Marie could wriggle through it or climb over it if she were to attempt to make another headlong dash to destruction. Even without the sides, in order to get into the road from the front steps, Marie would have been forced into a flanking maneuver, which would give us time to recapture her. Her best chance of escape would be to stow away in a laundry truck. So I gave myself a rest. During that time I came to realize how silly, inefficient, and expensive my fence design was.

This realization made it almost impossible to pick up my tools and finish the job. And this made the stand-alone front section look all the sillier. That's how matters stood in August when we came back from Connecticut.

Even though the playhouse ideas were bubbling and boiling inside my head, I had to put them on a back burner. Like a kid who has to put away one game before he starts another, I poked away at the silly fence without enthusiasm. I granted the chore a few grudging minutes every weekend, finally finishing it in October, at the tailend of good building weather.

Marie would get no tiny house that year. But I had all winter to make plans.

3. Sleeping Away

Something else besides the idea of building a playhouse came from that tough weekend in Connecticut: The Guys-Only Weekend.

On the last day of our visit, Betsy said to me, "You and the boys ought to spend a weekend together by yourselves. You're not getting much visiting done this way."

Even though Betsy had no more kept her high school friends than she had kept her baby teeth, she respected the friendship among us four boys who had clung together even though we'd all gone to different colleges and for years at a time lived thousands of miles apart. She didn't want my fatherhood to break up the pack.

I had almost knocked her over in my haste to forward the suggestion to my pals. Despite a little cold water thrown by their wives, the idea was warmly received by the boys.

That first Guys' Weekend would convene the following November in the Pocono Mountains in Pennsylvania because one of the guys, Russ, had access to a small house on a dismal little lake there.

I asked Russ, Tommy, and Doug to swing by for me late on the night of our departure so I'd get to put Marie to bed first. This had become a special time for Marie and me. After her bath I would put Marie into our double bed and chat with her a few minutes and then tell her a story. Then I'd rub her back or we'd snuggle while she went to sleep. Then I'd pick her up and carry her to her crib or "cage-bed," as it is known in our family. (We don't like to mince words;

everybody past the age of one knows that those bars are not for decoration.)

Actually, I've idealized the situation. That scenario is accurate only up to a point. In those days we were having sleep problems with Marie that were my fault. The dead of night was enlivened by all manner of activity, the centerpiece of which was Marie getting back into our bed and then expanding to queen-size—like a Japanese novelty flower dropped into water—to turn our nights into a hell of kicks and squirmings by a child unconsciously attempting to sleep diagonally.

I would remember those happy, childless nights when my head would hit the pillow and I'd be asleep before you could say "Feeling romantic tonight?"

When Betsy was still pregnant with Marie, on a visit to her sister Susan's family, we'd exchanged superior looks upon finding out that our youngest niece Heather never used her own bed, but slept with mom and dad every night. Words like "sick," "tacky," and "weak" came to my mind—and to Betsy's too, I suppose, because we didn't even have to talk about it; we were both of the same opinion concerning families that slept together all in a heap like a nest of nasty little mice.

Our own problems were inspired by memories of my own childhood. My fondest recollections of that time were of an activity that we called Lying Down. This was a bedtime treat administered by my dad. My brothers and I slept in the same room. At night, just before we deployed for Dreamland, Dad would lie down on one of our beds (it was a special honor for him to choose your bed) and review the day's events, talk about his childhood, or discuss life in general. Sometimes he'd make up stories about us, or about Chief Strongarm, an Indian superhero of his own creation. Other nights he'd tell war stories. (Dad was an Army veteran of World War II, having served with distinction, if not outright heroism, in the Illinois Theater of Operations.) Whether we were hearing about a pulling contest between the mighty chief and a locomotive, or the time a drunken sergeant's shoes were sucked off his feet in deep mud, these were magic moments.

As soon as my own little girl was old enough to appreciate a story, I revived the family tradition. As I'd hoped, this got to be a time for intimate chats and stories that at best were gems of spoken literature and at worst were thinly disguised propaganda encouraging her not to play with knives and to be polite at all times. And she lapped it up.

But when storytime was over and it was time to put her into her cage-bed, she resisted violently. A better parent would have held firm, but I hated to break the happy, peaceful mood I'd developed in the past half hour, and besides, what would it hurt if I let her fall asleep in the big bed and then carried her to the cage-bed?

Unfortunately, I have the gift of instant slumber whenever I lie still for more than sixty seconds. I could never wait out the ten minutes it took Marie to succumb, plus the additional thirty minutes it took her to sink into a sleep deep enough to withstand deportation to her own bed. So usually she'd remain in our bed half the night before my own sleep cycle and her movements made me lively enough to remove her.

Meanwhile, at the other end of sleeptime, my wife and I discovered that when our child awoke crying for Cheerios at five or six a.m. in the cage-bed, we could get another hour of sleep for her and for ourselves by letting her come back into the big bed.

Over a period of months, that brief span of time she spent in the crib got briefer and briefer. Until finally, to our shame, she was spending maybe an hour in her own bed and on some nights, no time at all.

Worse yet, the time she was spending in our bed, as hinted already, was far from cozy. In her sleep she'd thrash, gyrate, and thrust her limbs like a beleaguered ninja. Or digging her feet into the nearest adult body, she'd scramble up a rib cage like a fireman going up a ladder to perform a rescue. At dawn I'd feel like I'd been beaten and left for dead. I was earning the wages of permissive parenting.

So on that November night when I told Marie her story and rubbed her back to ease her into sleep, I was so excited by the prospect of a quiet night in Pennsylvania that I was able to outlast my unsuspecting tot. She was safely behind bars when the boys arrived and I gave Betsy a kiss of farewell and thanks.

The boys and I had a full three days of relaxation. Every day we drove into the nearby town of Honesdale where we ate in diners and drank in taverns. We shot pool and smoked cigars. At night we stayed in the house playing poker and watching movies on videotape, mostly informative stuff about women in prison. The only meal we ate in the house was a vat of chili brewed by Tommy. It looked a lot like the food from the cafeteria scenes in *Reform School Girls*.

Doug, a little more whimsical than the other two, lightened up the program somewhat by making a gourmet pear cake and showing a couple of black-and-white classics and Disney's *Pinocchio* on the VCR. And one afternoon, while Russ and Tommy were holed up in

Waslyk's Bar, Doug and I made a walking tour of Honesdale. At a variety store we bought Marie a plastic monster and a canister that goes moo when you turn it upside-down. At a seafood store we found a huge papier-mâché lobster costume on the floor in a corner and Doug got permission to put it on and go outside so I could take his picture.

Predictably enough, despite this succession of boyish delights, I was missing my little girl. She had recently coined the expression, "Love you too much," and the phrase haunted me in a poignant way that made me feel like there was something wrong with me, retreating to the edge of nowhere with these three guys who might possibly love me, but certainly not "too much."

By Sunday I was more than ready to resume a more useful role in society. Apparently the weekend in the Poconos had rehabilitated me more effectively than anything done to the women in *Slammer Girls* or *Caged Heat*. My goal was to get home in time to put Marie to bed. But a different contact sport intervened—football. First we watched the Steelers play the Oilers and when they were done, instead of shoving off, we had to see the Giants versus the Vikings. My impatience was apparent to the others, but Russ and Tommy are Giant fans and it was anybody's ballgame right up to the end, so we had to stay for every blessed down.

Though I resented every time-out and clock-stopping penalty, this kind of delay was nothing new. Ever since Marie was born, no family departure for any destination has ever been prompt. For me, the sports fans and their prolonged football game were just the manly equivalent of the child who befouls her diaper just as she's being herded into the car.

On the drive home I worried that Marie would give me the cold shoulder for running out on her. I'd heard of kids who do that to parents who leave them for much better reasons than a weekend of cigar smoking. But when I got home an hour before Marie's bedtime, our reunion was all I could have wanted. Hugs, kisses, and protestations of too much love. She was delighted with the toy monster I'd bought for her in Honesdale—a seven-inch-tall pink-and-orange thing made out of rubbery plastic, with a deep mouth you could stick your finger into.

Soon afterward, in the big bed, the monster had a starring role in the bedtime story. He came to life and played with Marie. In the dark beside me listening, the real Marie told me she wanted the monster to be bigger, so I had him grow to her size, but she wanted him bigger yet, so I had him grow to "a little bigger than Daddy" and this seemed to satisfy her. I try to be that kind of storyteller.

After the story, strong and refreshed from my weekend off, I felt inspired to make a new start on sleeping habits. "Now I'm going to put you in your cage-bed," I told Marie gently and to my surprise she said "Okay." And I carried her into her room, put her in bed and sat in a chair beside the bed for two minutes until she was asleep. (She didn't discover until the next night that this new procedure was to be permanent and we had a hellish hour of weeping and cajoling, but Betsy and I stood firm and have been sleeping a little better ever since.)

Maybe it was all those prison movies that emboldened me to put Marie into solitary confinement that first night home. Or maybe it was because The Warden and I had some serious catching up to do.

4. Sugar deprivation

The next month was a big one for Marie. On December 4 she celebrated her second birthday and got her first taste of birthday cake. It was her first taste of cake of any kind. Nor had she had any candy, cookies, ice cream, or soda pop.

Meanwhile, Betsy and I were living a lie. While we furtively stuffed ourselves with candy and ice cream, we'd been doing our best to raise a sugar-free child.

Of course, with sugar in just about all processed foods, that's almost impossible, but we steered her away from all the really obvious sources of sugar. This was one of Betsy's policy decisions; from the start she had gone about the business of motherhood in a scientific and enlightened manner. Her dedication to having a healthy baby was so deep that she'd given up caffeine and alcohol about three months before we even started practicing unsafe sex.

I'm grievously backward in matters of nutrition: I feel I'm being a health nut when I insist that the gasoline I use to start a barbecue fire is unleaded. But I support Betsy's mandates one hundred percent and I'm always ready to learn. For years we had been watching her little nieces and nephews go mental at family birthday parties. First I'd see the kids playing in a noisy but cheerful way. Then comes the ice cream and cake. My wife nudges me and whispers: "Watch this." And ten minutes later I'm in a horror movie— the kids are rushing around me in a frenzy, clawing at my legs, screeching and bellowing.

Betsy explained to me that another thing wrong with sugar is that besides delivering hammer blows to the pancreas, it replaces real food in the diet. She further informed me that in lab experiments done somewhere by someone, rats given the choice between sugared water and regular rat chow preferred the sweet water to the point of death by malnutrition. We were sitting in a restaurant with our snouts shoved into a pair of hot-fudge sundaes when Betsy withdrew hers long enough to present this scientific information. She imparted it without footnotes, although they might have been muffled by the whipped cream. But it sounds true, doesn't it?

Marie was asleep in her stroller about two feet away, never dreaming that such things as sundaes existed.

For the first couple of years, this was standard for us; we were as furtive as junkies when we indulged, eating most of the contraband while Marie was asleep. But when the timing was out of our hands, such as when we'd be visiting somewhere and cookies or cake would be served, Betsy would distract Marie with bananas or pieces of pineapple. Not knowing what she was missing, she'd readily eat the familiar stuff.

You could call it hypocrisy, but I call it trying to raise a new and improved generation. One that eats good, nourishing food. One that values things of the spirit. One that tells the time of year by the spiraling leaves of autumn, the sparkle of fallen snow, the delicate greens of spring, and the feel of clover under bare feet—not by candy corn, Christmas cookies, chocolate bunnies, and ice-cream cones. Me? I've already been ruined. Denying myself all these goodies would be pointless and cruel.

We kept Marie in the dark about cake and ice cream for as long as we could, hoping for the best. Some experts say that a child raised away from sugar won't develop a taste for it, but we knew early on that that wasn't happening. Marie could tell what contains sugar and ate all of it she could—salad dressing was a favorite beverage, and grapes awash in ketchup were a big delicacy.

During one of our secret binges (emptying a bag of chocolate-chip cookies, I think), with Marie napping upstairs in her cage-bed, I asked Betsy, "How long can we go on living this double life?"

"For as long as you like chocolate," she said.

But the fact is, we knew it was fast becoming impractical to steer Marie clear of sugary stuff without it becoming an inappropriately important element of her upbringing. So we relaxed the dietary laws for the sake of normalcy and Marie got a small piece of her own chocolate layer birthday cake. I'd like to report that she wasn't especially interested in it. But she ate it down to the last crumb and then licked the plate until Betsy took it away from her.

(Plate-licking, I remember from my own youth, is an effective way of asking for seconds in some households, but it didn't work on Marie's mom. Betsy may have retreated a few steps, but she hadn't thrown away her musket in headlong flight. With the Christmas season approaching, battle lines had to be re-formed pronto.)

5. Gifts received

Besides the stress and strain of eating as many Christmas cookies as possible to keep them out of Marie's hands, Christmas had gotten to be a trying time for me. It was the revelation factor.

When you open your gifts, you get a clear picture of what other people think of you. Which is why my big brother still gets me toy guns; to him I'll always be a ten-year-old, watching Saturday morning TV and mowing down toy soldiers with a hail of rubber bands.

And sometimes your gifts help show you what you've become. In the first years of our marriage, my wife, like an inexpert cannoneer, had been trying to zero in on what would be exactly the right gift for me. The sports jacket was a nice shot but it was wide of the mark and I seldom wore it. The tickets to the Broadway show missed, too. I went, but only to please her. These were gifts that she wanted me to want.

It took her a few years to adjust the trajectory and windage, but finally Betsy began scoring devastatingly direct hits. Pajamas. Bam! Bathrobe. Bam! Slippers. Bam! All things I liked and used daily. These lackluster accouterments landed dead-center into my lifestyle, blowing to bits my secret visions of myself as a sort of white-collar Davy Crockett.

So this year I was almost afraid to see what Betsy would fire my way. Another garment suitable for a hundred-year-old invalid? Not this time; she bought me a power saw! Something noisy and dangerous, something with which I would work my will upon defenseless lumber.

My wife apparently understood my new sense

of purpose. She recognized a jungle beast, crouched and preparing to spring, when she saw one, and had gifted me accordingly. This would not be just another summer of dabbling at fence-building and sitting on the front porch watching the paint peel. The paint would have to peel without my surveillance. I would be sawing and hammering loudly and manfully in the backyard, hewing a dream castle for my little girl.

However, even a man of action doesn't just jump into an important project with tools flailing. Careful planning had to come first. I'd gone back to the county library looking for plans and instructions for building playhouses. But, as was the case with the fence, the designs available didn't seem quite right. The playhouses were either chintzy plywood jobs or elaborate two-story structures. Something in between was called for.

John, a co-worker friend, had just built a workshop in his backyard, with the guidance of a skilled neighbor. He was bubbling over with the enthusiasm of the amateur and he took me under his wing, helping me plan the playhouse. Chatting after work, or drawing on scrap paper at lunchtime, he explained some basic construction techniques. While dispensing good advice, he kept pulling my ideas in the direction of something that was bigger and stronger and uglier than the little clapboard cottage I envisioned.

"John," I said, "I think you're making this playhouse into a copy of your workshop."

"Well, you oughta be practical," he said. "After a few years, Marie will outgrow the playhouse and then you should have it big enough so you can use it as a workshop or for storage."

That the tiny house would someday be abandoned by Marie and filled with old paint cans and other junk was unthinkable. "I don't care about that," I told John. Even if she did grow up, I felt pretty sure she'd mature into the kind of woman who'd still like to play with her dad in a tiny house. And if playing House with me was not completely fulfilling to her and she felt driven to get married and start a family of her own, the playhouse would be here for the wholesome pleasure of my grandchildren.

So I brushed aside his suggestions of a poured-concrete floor and finished-plywood siding with electrical service and there emerged board-by-board drawings of a pretty little playhouse, with floor space measuring six feet by five feet (just enough room for Marie and her dad to camp out in), with a front porch three feet deep. It would have three windows and two doors.

One Saturday in March the time to begin finally arrived. I assembled my drawings, measuring tape, level, shovel, and the six cinderblocks upon which the tiny house would sit. Before I got started, I sat down on the ground and drew Marie onto my knee for a formal announcement: "Marie, I'm about to start building your tiny house, but I have to tell you one thing first. Someday you might have a little brother or sister and you will have to share this tiny house with that little child. Okay?"

Marie's little moonface got red and its features twisted with anger. "No!" she yelled, and burst into tears.

At that point she had neither playhouse nor rival, but she understood what I was saying and, with the outraged instincts of an English earl, was invoking the rights of the firstborn.

6. Sick Ducks

I dug holes to set the cinderblocks at the right depths while Marie wandered around the yard waving sticks or picking grass. I divided my attention between her and the work at hand.

Every so often she'd come over and say, "Daddy, let's play."

"But Marie," I'd explain, "if we play, I'll never finish building your tiny house." She could see that, by her standards, I'd never finish the tiny house anyway. Here I had spent most of a Sunday afternoon and all I had to show for it were six cinderblocks partly buried in the ground. This wasn't even a weak start. It was no kind of start at all. Apart from the earthworms I had dug up and given her, I had wasted the afternoon.

Admittedly, work on the playhouse was slow. This was only partly because I didn't know what I was doing. The work was only done on weekends and it did not merit a child-care deferment the way floorwashing or lawnmowing would. In fact, Betsy, although supportive of the tiny house idea, saw my construction labor as only half an activity. A pastime like listening to the radio—something to be done while doing something else. And the something else was, invariably, minding Marie.

Naturally Marie was not interested in watching me work. But neither was I really eager to play her games. The affection was there, but my little companion and I did not have a lot of interests in common.

Before fatherhood, my idea of a good time was to sit down with a pot of coffee and a stack of books and magazines and systematically read a chapter or a page from each one in succession. Or, to the dismay of my wife, I would stay up most of the night watching movies of sex and violence on TV and then sleep most of the morning. These are not forms of recreation you can share with a tot.

We did have some common ground, though. We both liked to watch TV (I don't mind cartoons) and we both liked to play a game she devised called Sick Ducks.

Both of these activities were based on the sad fact, hinted at earlier, that I'm a fairly inert kind of guy. Even when I was young and wild, my idea of fun— horseback riding, motorcycling, canoeing, and hopping freight trains—centered on the notion of sitting there. Come to think of it, even the one parachute jump I made, though frightening, was about as passive a feat as can be found, and could have been performed by a sack of flour.

So we'd watch TV to the point of brain damage and then I'd read books to her, or I'd actually stand up on my hind legs and walk to the park with her to play on the swings, seesaw, etc. These are the kind of activities that will produce a smart, healthy, normal child and I forced myself to engage in them, getting some pleasure out of her enjoyment.

Because of my odd work schedule and because I'd sometimes stay up late to watch TV, I'd almost always be tired. So I'd opt for games that I could play while half asleep, or at least, while lying down.

My game of Howard Hughes' Last Day never caught on, but Sleeping Beauty (with a push from the Disney videotape) was popular, though sometimes I'd have trouble waking up after the kiss.

And that brings us back to Sick Ducks, a game that was justifiably abhorred by Betsy. In the game,

Marie was Donald Duck's nephew Louie and I would be another duck (usually Donald) and we'd lie down with a blanket pulled over our heads, either outdoors or in a bed. There was no dialogue in this game, only the occasional piteous whimper from one or the other of the sick ducks. There was precious little plot to our drama. Our condition neither improved nor worsened. Sometimes, however, the game would get to be too morbid even for me and, if I was feeling uncharacteristically peppy, I would take the role of the duck doctor and examine and treat my feathery pal.

Really it was a sick game by any standard and could have laid the foundation for real neurosis later on, so we cut back, never playing it in sunny weather or when Betsy was around.

But there were plenty of other activities to draw me away from building the tiny house. We blew soap bubbles, threw rocks into puddles, and ran through the sprinkler. Also, every once in awhile, just like the way malaria used to plague the diggers of the Panama Canal, an outbreak of the mysterious and debilitating duck disease would bring all work to a halt.

One Saturday evening about a month after breaking ground, I finished the floor. I pounded in the last nail and invited Marie up onto the foot-high platform I'd built. It was a sturdy framework covered by thick plywood for the main part of the house and treated boards for the porch. I put down my hammer and the two of us stomped around on the rock-solid floor for a couple of minutes. Then Marie got serious. "Daddy," she said, "I don't like the tiny house you're building."

"Why is that?" I asked, not overly concerned.

"It's too flat," she said.

7. Baby Bob and Baby Heather

My remark to Marie at ground-breaking ceremonies about a future sibling was not made just for the sake of controversy. Betsy and I had decided upon another exercise in procreation and that summer I successfully got Betsy "into trouble," as they used to say. (Betsy finds that expression offensive, but, having witnessed the rigors of childbirth, I find it accurate.)

Maybe I was just riling Marie to no purpose, considering that she was only two and a half at the time. But I've always tried to make Marie see me as fair and reliable. For example, whenever I would leave for work, I would announce it to Marie. Because this would make her cry, Betsy asked me if I couldn't just sneak out quietly. But I didn't want Marie to grow up not knowing whether her weasel of a dad had snuck off to work yet or was just momentarily out of sight.

With the playhouse, I didn't want to come off later as an Indian-giver when I eventually cut Child No. 2 in as a full partner. Maybe with my attempts at plain-dealing I was only upsetting her, but I felt that there would be a long-term beneficial effect.

This may sound like hollow piety, coming from a furtive eater of sundaes like myself. But that situation is different, although modern science has not yet perfected the instrumentation sensitive enough to measure that difference.

Anyhow, my remark to Marie was perhaps the least successful element of Project Baby. Betsy and I were like Procter & Gamble about to launch a new product. Our research-and-development department, working behind closed doors (when Marie took her afternoon nap), had done its part.

Now it was up to our marketing department to win acceptance. I'd read that Turkish emperors routinely strangled their younger brothers to eliminate competition for the throne. Whether you call that politics as usual or sibling rivalry, I call it sales resistance and I didn't want any of it in our house.

We had to create a demand. From a marketing point of view, we realized that to a big sister, a baby is kind of a white elephant. Stripped of all mystique, it's a doll you aren't allowed to play with. So we had to slather on the mystique.

Like all the best propaganda campaigns, ours was based on a couple of simple truths: That the baby would not just be Mommy's and Daddy's—it would belong to all three of us. And that despite minor functions as an alarm clock and a suction device, a baby's only important role is to be loved.

Marie's bedtime stories, which were already borderline public-service announcements, now became extended commercials for the joys and responsibilities of big-sisterhood. Lying there in the darkness, I invented two siblings for Marie—Baby Bob and Baby Heather. (These were just working titles.) Sometimes the babies could talk and sometimes not. But they could always get into trouble, and Marie would always rescue them. Many is the time Marie saved them from drowning in the Delaware River, which flows past our house. Usually Marie would prudently extend a long stick which the babies grabbed onto. In a wintertime classic, the babies escape from our house in the dead of winter and crawl through the falling snow, across the street and out onto the ballfield. Marie sees the open door and follows their tracks to find two pitiful little humps in the snow. But she digs them out, revives them, and, with the help of The Green Man (the World War I doughboy statue from in front of the nearby elementary school), carries them back home.

Whenever I was especially tired and needed to tell a really short story, I would have Baby Heather, the more impulsive of the two, crawl down the front walk, through the gate and out into the path of an onrushing red sportscar (driven by the same deranged hypothetical motorist who had inspired our safety fence). Marie manages to pull Heather out of harm's way just in time. As a reward for this act of heroism, Daddy gives Marie a cracker, which lends an air of realism to the tale.

On nights when I'd feel really strong, I'd unroll my masterpiece. In this one, the family is at the Philadelphia Zoo. Mom and Dad leave Marie to mind the babies in the stroller and go off, irresponsibly, to find coffee. The babies manage to climb out and then creep down into the zebra pit, where they laugh raucously at seeing horses in striped pajamas. This alarms the zebras who try to bite the babies. Marie by now sees what's going on, and in defiance of park rules, clambers into the pit and snatches the infants away so quickly that the zebras' snapping teeth close on empty air instead of tender baby flesh. Mom and Dad return and almost drop their cardboard cups of java when they see Marie and the babies climbing out of the pit. Marie is about to be punished for foolhardiness when a zoo attendant rushes up and tells of the daring rescue. He conducts the young heroine to an office where, according to zoo custom, she gets a special treat—a bowl of zebra chow with milk. It tastes like Cheerios, but whoever eats it breaks out in black stripes for the rest of the day. (Marie loved this story so much that we kept her under special guard whenever we visited the zoo.)

Meanwhile, wherever we went, Betsy would be pointing out babies and, when the situation warranted, as in visits to tiny cousins, we'd show Marie how gentle a big sister must be with babies. After one such visit Marie expressed a desire to go to the store right away to buy "teeny tiny clothes" for Bob and Heather. (Fat chance; the baby would wear hand-me-downs like every other second child and live to complain about it.)

One hot Saturday in July, Marie and I were sitting in the shade on the back porch of our house, gazing across about twenty feet of lawn to the unbuilt tiny house. It was only a wooden platform and a pile of 2-by-3s for the framework. I was wondering why I had decided to use 2-by-3s because that meant I had to buy 2-by-6s and cut each one in half lengthwise. My method of doing this called for Betsy to sit on one end of the board and I'd cut toward her with my new rotary power saw, putting her in the position of a silent-film heroine in a sawmill scene.

Marie, however, was wondering whether this hot weather might bring on an outbreak of sick-duck disease. "No," I said, with another look at my homemade 2-by-3s, "let's go to the movies."

Betsy, just over two months pregnant and feeling a little queasy, decided to stay home. We made it just in time to a matinee of Disney's movie about Br'er Rabbit. We found seats and Marie pointed to a couple of empties and said seriously, "Baby Bob and Heather can sit there when they come."

Apparently our campaign had peaked early. The customer was ready for delivery seven months ahead of the production schedule. If this had been a real business proposition, that would have been the moment to ask for a big down payment.

But there was nothing to worry about on that account. The real downside of the new baby would not become apparent to Marie until several hours after it was born. Marie and I had an exclusive one-to-one relationship. I know that I couldn't stand for her to suddenly acquire a new daddy, no matter what his endearing traits were. So I expected Marie would feel the same way when she'd see me lavishing love and attention on Baby Whoever. There was no way around the fact that Marie's monopoly was about to be busted in two and when she realized this, she'd know that her parents, especially her supposedly straight-tongued dad, had fooled and betrayed her.

Our public relations department, feeling nervous about the half-truths we'd been dispensing, was thinking that maybe a better approach would have been to say nothing about the pregnancy until about the fifth month. Then we could issue a brief statement:

"Marie, Mommy was stolen away by spacemen who implanted a new life form in her tummy. It will grow and grow and finally it will pop out. There's nothing we can do about it, except be nice to it. Above all, don't hurt it or make it mad, because it can shoot laser death rays out of its eyes."

It was one of the bolder and more creative concepts to emerge dripping from the shallow end of our corporate think-tank, but it came too late to be of any use.

8. Names

It was a typical Sunday afternoon on the construction site. After sawing two boards and driving seven or eight nails, I was taking a breather. Marie and I were sitting in the shade of our big maple tree drinking lemonade.

Betsy was nearby gardening. Before I'd met her, I'd thought gardening was a passive kind of pastime. You plant something and there it would remain undisturbed except for maybe some weeding, watering, or pruning.

But Betsy was constantly digging and transplanting, moving her plants all around our modest grounds in order to get them more room, more sun or less sun. Sometimes she moved her plants for aesthetic reasons, and sometimes she moved them out of mere restlessness. Hers or theirs, I couldn't tell. Being one of Betsy's plants was like being a fast-track executive for IBM or AT&T—they never knew where they'd be transferred to next. If we had the acreage I guess she'd be raising something that's easier to move around, like cattle.

Marie and I were trying to think up names for the baby and Betsy was trying to decide where to send the hydrangea bush.

"How 'bout 'Thumper'?" Marie suggested. She had already proposed Bambi, Dumbo, Dopey, and Pinocchio.

"How about 'Nicole'?" I suggested. Betsy didn't respond. Either she wasn't listening or she already knew I didn't mean it. Nicole was a good name, but I'd only said it to get the ball rolling. I'd feel silly having two daughters with French names. With just Marie, I felt that the Frenchness would not be noticeable. But two would be conspicuous and we'd be open to ridicule for trying to have French children. When my cousin Barry named his daughter Renée Michelle, I privately disapproved for that reason.

I also frown on giving children names that require accent marks not normally available on American typewriters. Why condemn a child to a lifetime of petty frustration for no good reason? (When Barry went back to the county records office with the birth certificate to make them add the proper accent mark to Renée, he should have gotten some inkling of what he'd done.)

Other variations from the norm are similarly punished, especially by unimaginative entities like the Army. My dad couldn't just get away with being Theodore Epstein—he had "no middle initial," so on official documents he was Theodore NMI Epstein. But even so, he fared better than a recruit that I heard about who insisted on his induction forms that only initials be used instead of his first and middle names. "R. only, B. only," he wrote and then had to serve two years as Pvt. Ronly Bonly Jones.

But even in civilian life you don't want to bestow names with nontraditional or alternate spellings. I don't want a child of mine forced to be constantly saying, "That's 'Michelle' with two l's," or "That's C-y-n-d-i." That time could be better spent mowing the lawn or discovering the cure for cancer.

Unisex names like Dale and Marion and Chris fall into a similar category, setting a person up for a lifetime of goofy mixups and low-grade jokes. A boy being assigned to a girls' gym class or a girl receiving a draft notice is only just so funny.

"How 'bout 'Flora'?" Marie asked. She had abandoned the Disney lineup and was putting forward the name of Babar the Elephant's daughter.

"I still like 'Kyra,' " Betsy said, as she began to dig up the hydrangea. I like a short name for efficiency's sake, but this favorite of Betsy's was one of those names that would have to be constantly explained, spelled, and pronounced for strangers.

"I'll go along with 'Kyra' for a girl, if you'll go along with 'Atom' for a boy," I said, pretty sure that this would be the last I'd hear of "Kyra." I was only bluffing, of course. I liked the name Atom—it was short, punchy and distinctive. It had a twenty-first-century flair to it, yet with a biblical echo. But it was another name that would waste a lot of time. Also a boy's name should be equally suitable for a baseball card or a physician's shingle. "Atom Epstein" would be right for neither, but it was a great name to wave at Betsy.

"How about 'Janice'?" Betsy asked, beginning to dig a hole about six feet away from the hydrangea's current location.

"No," I said. "There was a Janice in my fourth-grade class who wet her pants almost every day. It's a nice name and she was a nice girl, but I don't know, the pants-wetting kind of ruins it for me." The truth is that there was no Janice in my fourth-grade class. I just didn't like the name, so I was poisoning it. Either because of superstition that a child so named would become likewise afflicted or because she would from now on picture a pants-wetter whenever the name Janice was spoken, now there was no way Betsy would want to use it.

Because it was my trick, I'd never fall for it. A good name is a good name and if someone objectionable had it before, so what? A child breathes her own magic into a name and any previous owner will be quickly forgotten, no matter how disgusting or horrifying her traits or deeds."

Conversely I wouldn't name a son Herbert just on the strength of having known someone wonderful by that name. Chances are that the original Herbert would have been even more wonderful if considerate parents had given him a more appealing name.

I had used the name-poisoning ploy freely during all our child-naming exercises and perhaps overused it. Now Betsy said, " 'Janice'? Wait a minute. I thought it was Janet who wet her pants. And was that the same class that had Seth the spitter, Andy the biter, Vaughn the nose-picker and Marlene who grew up to be a nymphomaniac?"

Almost panicking, I said, "No, Vaughn was in my tenth-grade math class."

"Oh," she said, still suspicious, "with Donna who smelled bad and Benjamin who later shot his mother?"

"I forget," I said. Anxious to lead her away from my fictitious gallery of the incontinent, repulsive, and criminally insane, I suggested, "How about 'Eve'? Eve Epstein. I like that."

"Too provocative," said Betsy. "Do you really want to tempt fate that way?"

As I considered this, Marie saw an opening and demanded: "Why'd that girl wet her pants?" Like a dog under the dinner table, she wasn't about to miss any conversational crumbs that rolled down to her level.

"I don't know. I guess she was sick in some way and just couldn't help it," I said, not really wanting to get into it. "How about 'Caroline'?" I was looking for a name that would fit the kind of daughter I would hope to have—intelligent without being too serious, and feminine without being a sissy. Someone like Betsy.

"How about 'Sally'?" Betsy asked.

"That has possibilities," I said. "Let's remember that one." Marie said she liked that name, too.

We turned our attention back to boys' names. If Marie had been a boy, she'd have been named Alec. It would have been logical to save this extra name for the second pregnancy, but for some reason we now decided Alec sounded pretentious, so we scrapped it. In those pre-Marie days, my bluff name had been Wild Bill. I used to insist that I wanted to name a son Wild Bill, even though I knew full well that such a son would be sure to be a trial and an embarrassment growing up, and as an adult he would probably visit me once a month only to beat me up and take my Social Security check.

Which reminds me of Freedom Rose. In the spring of '76 I was on a Tucson, Arizona, city bus sitting beside a pretty girl with an ugly scar on her wrist. I struck up a conversation with her which was easy because she, like me, believed her life story to be too rich a treasure to be kept private.

In the course of a fifteen-minute chat, I learned that she was sixteen and that a couple of years previous she and her boyfriend had run away from home. They had hitchhiked as far as Oklahoma when the boyfriend "got into a fight" with the driver and tried to shoot him. The bullet penetrated the girl's wrist. After she got out of the hospital, the authorities brought her back to Arizona, though her boyfriend's presence was required in Oklahoma for a while.

Besides the scar, she brought back a souvenir of their adventure—a baby who was born about nine months after her return. The girl named her baby Freedom Rose. The court awarded custody of the baby to the mother of my young bus companion. Apparently Freedom Rose's grandma figured that living up to a handle like Freedom Rose was a likely way to become a second-generation runaway/gunshot victim. So the first thing she did was to change the baby's name to Helen.

Unlike Helen's mom, I knew deep down that any creative impulses must be stifled for the sake of all concerned. A name is nothing more than a garment for a child to wear—thoughtful parents will steer past the clown suits and tuxedos and find something all-purpose and tasteful, halfway between plain and fancy. The best name is not a big sign that must be carried everywhere and explained forever, nor is it a strong dog on a leash that will pull its owner in unwanted directions.

Thinking along traditional lines, the idea of naming a son after myself appealed mightily to my vanity. When I was in college, my girlfriend suggested that if we ever got married and had sons they should be named Richard Epstein 1 and Richard Epstein 2. But we disagreed on almost everything else, so our romance did not terminate in marriage.

The more moderate course of naming a son Richard Epstein, Jr., had been rejected by both Betsy and myself. The arguments against it were overpowering:

1. Anyone acquainted with the old *I Love Lucy* TV show would be calling him Leetle Reeky.
2. A name should be picked on its merits. Using a name because it's the father's is as wise as hiring your brother-in-law.
3. It would make for continuous mixups of mail

and phone calls. (As a newspaper editor I would frequently find indignant fathers and sons pointing to the Jr. or Sr. at the ends of their names or at contrasting middle initials and berating me for sloppy work. I never said it, but the really bad job had been done in the naming.)

4. Like a squealer in the federal witness-protection program, each child should get a fresh new name and be set free of any bad blood associated with the old name. Let the boy make his own enemies.

5. When you "junior" someone, at one stroke you deny his individuality and diminish him. It tells Richard Epstein, Jr.: "You are your father, only less." And that wouldn't be enough. (If I could name him Richard Epstein Plus it would be more positive, implying that this is a new and improved model, most of the bugs having been worked out of the original Richard Epstein, which had been rushed through production and put on the market prematurely.)

6. Don't be misled by a man who insists on the Jr. at the end of his name. That guy must really love being a junior, one might think. But the chances are that he clings to that Jr. because it's the only part of his name that he can truly call his own. Pathetic.

7. If my son would grow up to be a huge success it would be nice to bask in his reflected glory. But things don't always work out for the best. How would you like to be Lee Harvey Oswald, Sr.? (Not that I believe a word of the Warren Commission Report.)

Another danger in naming boys lies among the names, such as Kevin, Todd, and Gary, that are good for a child but not so good for an adult.

I know a man named Todd who is a six-foot-two father of three and the pastor of a church and he goes around looking like he ought to be spanked. I think if he were named William or James he wouldn't grin quite so sheepishly nor would he scuff his shoes on the pavement when he walks. A long time ago I rode freight trains from Seattle to Chicago with two guys named Gary and I think their names had something to do with their willingness to act so irresponsibly. (My own reasons have something to do with my calling myself Rick; but I'm not locked into it—I can move up to Richard whenever I feel ready.)

"How 'bout 'Wheezer'?" Marie asked. That was our cat's silly name and it had been suggested several times already.

"Samuel might be a good name," Betsy said, dragging the hydrangea over to the new hole. And so it continued. Whenever we were brainstorming, we always seemed to be in the eye of the storm.

When trying to name Marie, our negotiations had taken the full nine months. On Betsy's due date I phoned the hospital to find out what they do if a child is born and a name cannot be agreed upon. (The hospital just fills in the first name Baby on the birth certificate and leaves it to the parents to substitute a more specific name later.)

We were delighted when we stumbled onto "Marie." It was short, easy to spell, and traditional though not overused. Also it passes the all-important schoolyard-rhyme test.

Betsy and I had been more extravagant in the

middle-name department. We loaded Marie down with two—Matheson and Westlake—the maiden names of my mother and Betsy. A little outlandish perhaps, but a middle name is like a tattoo on your backside. It's always there, but it's up to you who sees it.

For that reason, the space between first and last name can be put to many uses. It can be used to appease a spouse who is aiming to hang an inventive name on an innocent child. It can be used to flatter a rich uncle or to placate a dad who is intent on a namesake. A well-wrought middle name can also be your child's lifeboat in case she decides your first choice is unseaworthy.

I'm afraid we didn't give Marie much help in that regard, but at least we didn't just casually throw in an Ann the way you toss an extra pair of socks into a suitcase. Betsy has Ann for a middle name and she claims it's a good middle name because it sounds good with other names. I say you want a genuine name, not a mere conjunction as in "ham an' eggs" or "rock an' roll." Having warmed up with Marie M. W. Epstein, I wanted to really shovel in the middle names for Child No. 2. Five or six would be about right. But Betsy said Matheson Westlake went as far as she'd care to go in that direction and those names would be equally suitable the second time around. And that was that. Thus our energies were directed back to the front end of the name.

For most parents, the selection of a name is the first and last situation over which they are in total command. By the time Marie was two and a half we'd begun to realize this. Maybe that's why Betsy and I were making the most of it, borrowing name books from the library, checking family records, and even studying the closing credits of movies and the police log of the weekly newspaper—examining any source rich in names.

The naming sessions were frequent and went on into the winter, each one more or less productive. The afternoon session just described was one of the more fruitful ones. Its net results: Sally as a maybe; Kyra, a threatening contender, skillfully neutralized by Atom; an advance of six feet to the north by the hydrangea; and a little practice for Marie at being robbed of her parents' attention by the baby.

9. Nails

For Marie, the most appealing things about building the playhouse were the nails and other makeshift toys the project involved. She had plenty of real toys strewn all over the yard, plus a live cat if she could catch it, and there was lots of fun dirt and grass underfoot, but she wanted to play with the things I was playing with.

At first I tried to keep her out of the nails for safety reasons. By that time Marie had quit putting foreign objects into her mouth, so I wasn't afraid she'd swallow the nails. I was afraid she'd hurt herself on the points, but that never seemed to happen so I let her live it up.

She just liked to sit on the wooden platform that would be the floor and take the nails out of the bags one by one and put them into piles. Then she'd put them one by one into other piles. Sometimes I'd catch her dropping the nails through the spaces I'd left between the boards that would form the floor of her front porch. I tried to limit this action because any nails dropped down there could not be retrieved.

Besides the nails, Marie liked to play with the level, waggling it around to see its little bubble in yellow liquid move, and whacking the ground with it when she got tired of the bubble. The container of blue powder, for the chalkline, was another source of amusement as she shook it until she and her surroundings were all blue.

My retractable metal measuring tape was popular, too. She'd pull out about thirty inches' worth and run around the yard, holding it by the tail. Since I had little confidence and had to measure each board every few minutes, Marie's interest in my tape measure developed into an ongoing contest. Her nail-arranging also tended to slow things down because I had to negotiate for each one as I needed it. For my purposes, the chalkline powder was the best plaything for Marie, partly because I seldom needed it and partly because if she got blue enough, Betsy would quit gardening and take her off my hands for a while to clean her up.

It was about this time that Marie was visiting her Uncle Jim and heard a tape of Billie Holiday singing "Am I Blue." Possibly thinking it was about someone who'd been fooling around on a construction site, she asked her uncle, "Why she blue?"

Jim, trying to keep it simple, answered, "Because a man hurt her and made her feel sad."

Not seeing what this had to do with chalkdust, but alarmed that one person would hurt another, Marie asked, "What her mommy and daddy say about that?"

Jim had no ready answer and Marie was left a little confused about that song in particular and blueness in general. Thereafter she regarded the chalk container with suspicion and seldom gave it more than a passing shake.

My worst moment in building the playhouse came when I realized I had cut the plywood for the roof too small. Without thinking, I'd made it the same size as the floor. But roofs have to be a little bigger in order to keep rain from dripping down inside the walls. After I'd put on the clapboard siding, my walls would actually extend half an inch beyond the protection of the roof. Think of a very fat man standing under an umbrella so tiny that it channels the rainwater down inside his shirt-collar, and you have the essence of my roof problem.

I'm not an emotional builder, but when I comprehended my mistake I looked quickly around to make sure Marie wasn't watching and then I threw my hammer at the ground as hard as I could. Then I sat down on the grass in despair. This tiny-house project plainly meant more to me that it would to a person in top mental condition.

Marie came toddling over pretty soon to find out why Daddy looked like he was about to cry and why the hammer was buried neck-deep in the ground. I told her, "Daddy needs a hug." She complied and my perspective seeped back. I was ashamed of my self-pity, but kind of proud of my exhibition of temper. (I later boasted of it to Betsy who didn't believe me.)

By adding strips of wood to the edges of the plywood I was able to do an adequate job of expanding the roof. Crisis averted. I would be covering my mistakes with tarpaper and shingles, so no one need ever know.

Working as many as four hours per weekend and putting in as much as eight minutes of uninterrupted labor at a time, by September I had the playhouse finished, clapboard siding and all. Marie had been busy too, as future archaeologists will attest when they excavate under the little porch and find a nail stockpile big enough to affect compass readings taken within one hundred yards of the tiny house.

I put down my hammer and called Marie over from where she was drawing in the dirt with a stick and announced, "Marie, your tiny house is finally finished." I guess I expected her to throw her arms around my neck and squeal, "Oh! Daddy! I just love it!" But instead she handed me her stick and said, "Draw me a doggie."

It pains me to report this, but Marie never warmed up to her playhouse the way I'd hoped she would. She likes it but she doesn't love it. In good weather she'll entertain visitors in the playhouse and she takes a certain amount of pride in it because other kids covet it. She's like a nineteenth-century cannibal king, aggrandized by the ownership of an umbrella. And it's excellent PR for me. When other couples visit us, wives look critically at their husbands and I know they are comparing them unfavorably to me. Wives have never done this before and I like it.

I suppose that from the start the playhouse was more something I wanted to give Marie than it was something that she wanted to have. For sheer enjoyment, Marie, even now at age five, would prefer to take a few stuffed animals and hole up behind the couch than go outside and play in her kid-size house. Or she and a playmate will build their own "house" by stacking scrap lumber and tree branches against our woodpile and weaving ropes through it, creating what looks like a collection of flotsam deposited by receding flood waters. Meanwhile her trim, lovingly crafted playhouse gathers cobwebs thirty feet away, apparently waiting for my grandchildren.

Does this bother me? Yes.

10. Wheezer

As summer drew to a close our cat ran away.

Wheezer was a small, gray, tiger-striped cat I'd adopted about the time Betsy and I were first going together. Wheezer had strayed into an ideal situation. She was the child who Betsy and I were meaning to have someday. Wheezer was petted, combed, fed royally, and photographed frequently. A companionable creature, she learned to recognize the distinctive engine sound of the VW bug I was driving in those days and she'd run to meet me when I drove up. Betsy and I would take walks and Wheezer would tag along.

In the winter, to keep her from sleeping on the stovetop over the pilot light, I got Wheezer a heating pad and made her a bed of old towels on top of it. I even tacked up pictures of zoo lions and circus tigers at her eye-level near her bed. Our house and the surrounding fields and woods were prime mousing territory and Wheezer delighted in the hunt and the ensuing meal. The sight and sound of the celebratory feasting were disgusting to us, but Betsy and I believe that a cat should be permitted to be a cat so we tried to be understanding.

Maybe the best part of Wheezer's lifestyle was the cat door I made for her. I put a hole in the kitchen wall and built a door that swung outward and upward for an easy exit. To get in, Wheezer had only to step on a little flat board in front of the cat door. Her weight on that board would pull a string that went around a pulley and was tied to the bottom of the cat door. The pull on the string opened the cat door right in front of her nose and in she went. This arrangement gave her the kind of independence that cats cherish.

With a heaping bowl of dry Kat Krispies to supplement her catch-of-the-day, we could go away for days at a time and Wheezer would be fine.

But Wheezer's heaven-on-earth was not to last. When Marie was born all our attention was diverted to the baby. The petting and combing ended. We still fed her, but we no longer thought to buy her cat candy or to pour cod-liver oil on her Krispies.

Once, when Betsy had to be away for an afternoon, she left me and the baby alone with a bottle of human milk that she'd extracted with a pump of some kind. After Marie had tanked up, there was about an ounce left over. Not enough to save. Partly to show kindness to our neglected cat, and partly to add to the sum of scientific knowledge, I poured it into a bowl and put in on the floor for Wheezer.

I began to have misgivings as soon as I put the bowl on the floor. Was I leading our cat toward the development of bizarre and inappropriate tastes? How would I explain to Betsy why Wheezer was following her around the house meowing and jumping up on her shoulder trying to get into scoring position? But the thin milk did not appeal to Wheezer. She gave it a sniff and slunk disappointed back into the shadows.

Soon poor Wheezer's quality of life was to be eroded even further. So far, Wheezer had been the only pet in the neighborhood, except for a few well-leashed dogs.

Now suddenly our street abounded in cats. There

were about six of them and they soon learned that Wheezer's easy-to-operate cat door was the twenty-four-hour-a-day key to free food and good times. If Wheezer was at home, a good, screaming, claws-out catfight could be enjoyed. If she was out, there was a floor to pee on, as if to say, "Sorry I missed you."

The predawn catfights always hurled us into shocked and angry wakefulness. I used to keep a badminton racket beside the bed. I'd grab it and run down the stairs, hoping for a chance to discipline the intruder. But by the time I got to the foot of the stairs I'd hear the hollow pop of the cat door closing behind the retreating interloper.

I rigged up a rope from the cat door up to our bedroom window, so when a fight broke out, I could tie the door shut and trap the cat inside the house. Then I would go downstairs and teach it a lesson.

The rope trick worked. With the cat screams that had awakened me still resounding through the house, I went downstairs and turned on the lights which illuminated a terrifying scene. A panicked black cat, robbed of its exit, was screeching like a demon from hell and running wild in our kitchen. It seemed to be racing along the stone walls, centrifugal force enabling it to get a footing on the vertical surfaces, like one of those thrill-show motorcyclists. Wheezer was cowering in the bathroom. All thoughts of discipline vanished. I threw open the back door so the hellcat could escape. Then I joined Wheezer in the bathroom.

The next day I nailed the cat door shut and caulked it tight. From then on, poor Wheezer had to beg to get in or out. And when we went away overnight, unless it was the dead of winter, Wheezer became an outdoor cat, like it or not.

Other than food, some door-opening service, and

the occasional perfunctory pat on the head, Wheezer got no attention—until Marie was old enough to pull a tail. Marie loved the cat and her first word was "Wheezer" but the manifestations of her affection were usually painful or degrading.

Wheezer did not like being slobbered on and smeared with banana pâté or having her limbs and tail pulled and twisted. Despite our remonstrations, Marie in her enthusiasm didn't so much play with the cat as she played the cat. Like an accordion. Wheezer somehow endured it for more than a year. She finally ran away from home, but she did it in a peculiar way. She disappeared in late September. When she stayed missing for several days, we figured maybe she was dead. But after two weeks, she reappeared briefly. I was writing checks in the kitchen when I heard Marie's gleeful cry: "Wheezer's back!"

While Marie chased Wheezer in circles around the yard, I found a can of cat food. Then Betsy rescued the cat from Marie and allowed only some well-supervised petting while I put the dish down in front of the prodigal.

But Wheezer wasn't especially hungry and we noticed that she was as plump as we'd ever seen her. Apparently Wheezer had found a nice place for her two-week vacation.

An hour later, after Betsy had evicted Wheezer from her garden and Marie had cheerfully terrorized the cat with a toy broom, Wheezer disappeared and hasn't been seen since. It was as if she'd come back to confirm that her life with us was as bad as she'd remembered and it was.

In an unguarded moment a couple of months later Betsy observed, "I guess Wheezer has found a family she likes better than us." This remark wounded Marie and she'd repeat it mournfully to anyone who she thought might be wondering why we had no cat.

Marie's sense of loss and injury was further revealed months later when she made her first crayon drawings that were representational, rather that scribbles. At first she only drew cats. Each cat's head had pointed ears and chin (like a valentine heart drawn without curves) and no body but four stick-legs extending down from the head and a quick horizontal stroke for the tail. She drew lots of these cats and once she'd mastered them, she drew them engulfed in red and yellow flames with gray smoke spiraling upward. There was no mistaking what it was a picture of. Marie confirmed that these were burning cats but she'd make no further explanation. (Some artists, especially young, angry ones, hate to explain their work.) Over the period of two weeks she churned out about seven of these disturbing pictures and then turned her talents into more pleasant avenues.

It's pretty safe to guess Marie was simply venting or processing the violent feelings instilled when her cat abandoned her. But all the same, if Wheezer is smart she'll stay gone this time.

11. Bullies or sissies

With November came the Second Annual Guys-Only Weekend. One of the guys, Tommy, had moved to St. Petersburg, Florida, in the intervening year and he agreed to host the four-man convention in his apartment.

A November weekend in the Poconos is nothing

to envy; Florida sounded considerably more enticing. But Betsy, who likes beaches a lot more than I do, managed to take this escalation of the guys' weekend in stride. In fact, she had tried to put together a girls' weekend in Bermuda with a couple of her friends, but they had begged off for reasons financial, marital, or maternal. She could only blame herself for having the wrong kind of friends.

What should have been a relaxing time with pals turned out to be a moderately unpleasant exercise in consciousness-raising. The seeds of disaster had been sown during the Pennsylvania weekend. Recalling the things we'd done then—drinking beer, smoking cigars, playing poker, watching football—the theme for the St. Pete weekend turned out to be "manliness." It was meant to be all in fun, but the joke outlived its funniness by a couple of days.

The tone was set on the first day when we were lying on the beach, smoking cigars and drinking tequila, when one of the boys posed the question for each of us to answer, "What's the manliest thing you've ever done?"

From there, the conversation evolved into ranking the four of us according to classical standards of manliness. (For our purposes, manly and macho mean the same thing. For example, being a loving father and a steady provider counts against you. But getting drunk and smashing windows is worth major points.)

A good index of manliness is how often you've had a loaded gun pointed at you. For Russ, it was at least three times. I'd never had a gun pointed at me, but it is to my credit that in wilder days I had been present when a .38 had been pressed into Russ's face by a Burlington Northern railroad guard in a Seattle freightyard. However, I lost manliness points because

I had talked the guard into letting Russ go; a truly manly man would have dared the guard to shoot the both of us.

Sexual exploits also counted heavily, provided that no unmanly sentiment was involved, and Russ cleaned up there as well. He also led the league in drinking, fistfights, and athletic prowess.

Thanks to adventures I'd had in the 1970s, I was ranked a distant No. 2 with protests and reservations expressed by the others. Tommy (No. 3, avoiding last place by virtue of his no-frills lifestyle and love of pro sports) pointed out that although I was the only father in the group, my child was a girl—worth less than nothing in the manliness sweepstakes. (To a manly man, the father of a girl or young woman is an object of special contempt.) But it was conceded that if the baby due in March turned out to be a boy I would pick up a couple of points.

Doug's remarks were even more pointed. He had nothing to lose—his taste for Perrier and his habit of settling problems by taking them to court had earned him the No. 4 spot. Lying there on the beach, prudently applying sunscreen to his pale flesh, he charged that I hadn't done anything manly for years "even though Rick sort of threw himself off a cliff there for five or six years, he did it to overcompensate for his real inner wimpiness."

His charge was fairly accurate, but luckily for me, manly men are not going to listen to a guy who bakes pear cakes and has himself photographed in a lobster suit. I had a copy of *Miami Massacre* (volume five in the Executioner series) at my side and I was just about to try for extra points in the literary-taste category when my wristwatch started beeping to remind me that it was time to put more quarters in the parking meter and my claims to manliness took a body blow. My No. 2 status was mocked and challenged for the rest of the weekend.

After feeding the meter and visiting the beachside snack bar, I failed to give adequate answers to questions about the "babe" in the pink bathing suit who was ahead of me in line. I was accused of failing to check her out properly.

I was further derided for phoning my wife and daughter every night at six o'clock: "It's wimpy enough to call your wife, so at least call at midnight and wake her the hell up," was the general sentiment. And when, after eating Tommy's specialty of the house (burned chili), I asked if anyone had any Alka-Seltzer, I was called "a fruit" and a box of baking soda was thrust into my hands for my indigestion.

My low point came when I took the wheel to drive home after a night of gambling at the greyhound races, which made it apparent to even the drunkest of the guys that I was the only sober one. (I could've defended myself by pointing out that a true drunken manly man would insist upon taking the wheel, but I kept that thought to myself.)

I probably would have been stripped of No. 2 honors except that it would have touched off terrible wrangling between Nos. 3 and 4 and our weekend would have been made even worse.

When Sunday afternoon came and it was time to fly north, we were all pretty sick of each other and there was some doubt as to whether a Third Annual Guys-Only Weekend would be necessary. We all came away feeling that we'd spent the weekend in ill-fitting straitjackets.

After a joyous reunion with Marie and Betsy, I was able to accommodate other sectors of my soul that had been frustrated in St. Pete and to play a part for which no one would dispute my fitness—that of Morty the Mouse, Mickey's nephew. It was with great relief that I tucked a length of curly, black phone cord into the back of my pants for a tail.

The stifling feel of Manliness Weekend returned the next day when I spent my lunch hour shopping for a tricycle for Marie's birthday. I found the toy store's bike department and was confronted by the "Li'l Dominator." Believe it or not, that was the name of a particular breed of bicycle. It was small, but it was painted an ominous black and had the wicked, blunt look of an automatic pistol. Need I say that this was a boy's bike? I'd go a step further and say this would be the perfect first bike for a future wife-beater.

The girls' bikes were nearby. A girl could have "The Mermaid" in pastel green with white tires or "The Princess" in a delicate pink.

What happens, I wondered, when the Li'l Dominator and The Princess approach each other at full tilt on the sidewalk? My guess is that when the dust clears there'll be a quivering heap of pink ruffles and twisted metal on the lawn and a black form receding into the distance, laughing scornfully.

I looked further and managed to find a similar orientation among the tricycles, but there were a couple of them that looked as though they were designed for generic people—normal human beings—instead of specialized bullies or sissies. I bought a bright red one that seemed to be designed for low-speed fun, not sexual politics.

Betsy and I had discovered the same phenomenon when we went to buy Marie a winter jacket. We could either get a pink one with bows on it, or a black one emblazoned with the words "Wrecking Crew." When I asked the saleswoman if she had any jackets in green or orange, she looked at me as if I'd requested something unnatural.

There are few places to hide from what seem to be aggressive efforts to groom my daughter for a life as a trembling fern. As the weather grew colder, we were spending more time in front of the TV, often communing with a variety of cartoon characters. Marie and I enjoy the Disney classics, but you don't have to be a raving militant to discern the male domination that pervades the short subjects and feature films.

Have you ever really taken note of what Minnie Mouse and Daisy Duck are all about? Not much. They wear high heels, flirt with Mickey and Donald, respectively, and that's about it. Meanwhile, Donald is busy getting caught in a dog-washing machine, humiliating himself in a talent show, being abused by his nephews, or flying a defective airplane. True, Donald usually doesn't have a good time, but at least he's got more on his frenzied mind than whether Daisy will like his new hat.

And in those feature-length movies, Snow White is just a variation on the housekeeper/sex object; Cinderella is the traditional housekeeper/martyr, except she achieves this status *before* marriage; the Little Mermaid is an empty vessel without Prince Eric; the mother Dalmatian is a wimp; the mom Aristocat uses her allure instead of her wits to get help for herself and her kittens; Lady is in distress until Tramp comes along and shows her which end is up; and Sleeping Beauty just lies there spending quality time with Mr. Pillow while the Prince is leaping ravines, hacking his way through an enchanted brier patch and slaying a fire-breathing dragon. He kisses the sleeper who wakes up and says, oh, did I miss anything, and the next thing you know, they are dancing in the sky.

A recurrent message is that marriage is the happy ending to a woman's tribulations.

My sister-in-law Karen must have had a headful of those fantasies when, just out of college, she told Betsy, "Maybe I'll just get married and let my husband take care of me."

If Marie ever comes out with anything like that, I won't have to worry. Betsy will explain to her that marriage is not so much like being Sleeping Beauty dancing on clouds as it is like being Rip Van Winkle— you follow a strange man into unknown terrain and the next thing you know you're twenty years older and you've got one hell of a headache.

It was just about this time that Marie's "all-boy" cousin Dave was over to visit. He was five years old to her three. They went upstairs to play House. Twenty-five minutes later, when we hadn't heard a word from them, curiosity got the better of me and I went up to investigate. I looked in upon an unusual domestic scene. Marie, putting a towel over her shoulders like a shawl, said, "Okay, I'm ready to go to the party."

Her boy husband, lying face down on the floor, gasped, "I can't. I'm stabbed."

Not that I want Marie to cast herself as the victim of a knife assault, I wondered nevertheless whether little girls are just naturally inclined toward the mundane and safe while little boys are just naturally preoccupied with violence and mayhem. Does our culture simply hurry our kids along paths laid out by nature or does it brutally press them into limited and crippling roles they must play for the duration? Who can say? Certainly not young Dave. All he knew for sure was that one minute he was fine and the next minute: Unngh! Stabbed!

12 · Swirling sea of toys

As the holiday season approached, I got the feeling Noah must have had after twenty rainy days into the flood when the forecast called for twenty more of the same.

I'm talking about toys. Every room seemed to be awash in a shifting sea of toys. A fresh deluge on Christmas morning could make our house unlivable.

A household's toy mix is as distinctive as a fingerprint. Ours consisted of big wooden blocks, old plastic Civil War soldiers, books, crayons, coloring books, drawing paper, hand puppets, dolls, ribbons, puzzles, plastic boats and cars, and about three cubic yards of stuffed animals. That December, in advance of Christmas, Betsy announced to friends and relatives a moratorium on stuffed animals for Marie.

A census taken of her creatures at the time includes: a dozen bears, five dogs, three elephants, three penguins, three rabbits, two cats, a squirrel, a duck, a turtle, a frog, an ostrich, a reindeer, an alligator, a mammoth, and that's not counting her human dolls, puppy slippers, a real fox skin with glass eyes and a clip jaw that used to be an item of someone's apparel, and a plush Santa the size of a kindergartner.

From a wildlife management standpoint, the problem is that, unless you have a pet dog, stuffed animals have no natural enemies, no predator who eats them up. So they multiply unchecked. (For the exact equation take six uncles, five aunts, and three grandparents. Multiply that number times one birthday and one Christmas. From this you can pretty well project the growth in population, realizing that for every one of those relatives who fails to come forward with a stuffed animal, a well-meaning friend of the family will. Also, don't forget to factor in Easter, when rabbits and chickies make a strong showing.)

The moratorium is a valid toy-husbandry technique, but really it was too little too late. A more ruthless parent would have waited until Marie was napping, and then put ten or twenty of her creatures into a box, brought them into a toy store and set them free.

The wife of a friend of mine used a terroristic variation on this deportation gambit. To punish her daughter's insubordination, she seized a pair of highly prized figurines, a rabbit and a raccoon, and returned them to the store. But this was more of a temporary hostage situation than a gamelands management practice. The child repented and the creatures were ransomed, so what little respite the family got from clutter was hard-won and fleeting.

To try to thin Marie's herd, we implemented a sort of colonization program. One contingent of animals (two bears and a squirrel) stays at my father's house, and another group (two penguins and a bear) is kept at my in-laws' house. Other animals do time in Betsy's car, usually remaining in it for several months at a stretch.

(I don't know if the car animals are there on purpose, though; things have a way of staying in Betsy's car for a long time. You might not believe this, but she still has her bridal bouquet in her glove compartment from eight years ago! What with all the automotive vibrations and rummaging for maps and documents, lots of the foliage has chipped off, but it's basically still there—a mummified tangle of wire, brown roses, and yellow ribbon—reminiscent of the old spinster's mouse-eaten wedding cake in *Great Expectations*. Incredible, but true.)

Naturally we never buy stuffed animals for Marie. She was intrigued by the pre-Christmas displays of computerized animals that recite stories while moving their mouths and blinking their eyes. But she hadn't yet figured out that grownups are supposed to buy them and take them home for their children. Betsy had convinced her that these creatures reside in the stores and if you want to be with them, you had to visit the store. You could no more buy them than you could purchase the animals in a zoo.

Another space-saving method we borrowed from museum curators. We warehouse boxes of artifacts in the attic, and bring them down for public enjoyment on a rotating basis. This approach sometimes takes some perseverance. In January when we kidnap her huge Santa, Marie demands and achieves his return several times before he is finally allowed to spend his off-season where he belongs.

A similar way to artificially limit the number of toys in circulation is the time-capsule approach. Just fill a cardboard box full of toys and stick it in the back of the child's closet where it won't be found for a generation or so.

But let's not kid ourselves. Turnover is the key to the toy crisis. That's why snow is the best toy. Children can sculpt it, build with it, slide on it, and throw it. Best of all, you won't be stumbling over it for the next ten years.

I used to love to play in snow, but the older I get, the colder and wetter snow gets. When a December storm dumped a couple inches of snow here, I would have gladly waited indoors for it to go away. But I forced myself to take Marie outside and help her build a snowman. I plan far ahead. I want Marie to grow up thinking winter is fun. Otherwise she might decide to spend her adult years in the sunny South leaving me in New Jersey, missing her grievously. So with freezing extremities and running nose, I drag her around town on a sled, let her pelt me with snowballs and even lie down to make snow angels. Great fun, eh, Marie? Nothing like this in Florida!

One special feature of making a snowman in our backyard is the things you find. Rolling a snowball along the ground, in hopes that it will get bigger, forgotten toys of summer are constantly appearing on the top of the snowball, embedded there en route to temporary entombment inside Frosty. When the next thaw comes, a sad huddle of little Fisher-Price people and unbreakable dinosaurs is discovered lolling in the slush along with my old corncob pipe and a limp, discolored carrot.

Anyhow, until snow is available in stores, whenever anyone asks what Marie wants for birthday or Christmas I holler "Art supplies!" Paint, colored chalk, crayons, and Play-doh all have a serious impact on household tidiness, but they are all wonderfully consumable. With proper encouragement of the young artist, there is no accumulation, provided that you throw away any crayon that gets to be shorter than one inch and pieces of chalk smaller than a pea.

Bubble-blowing fluid falls into this category, too. As an artistic medium it tends to be limiting, but at least there is no residual problem of what to do with the finished masterpieces, as with paintings. In that regard you have to be tough about limiting your art collection or you'll lose any ground you've gained. I keep only the very best of Marie's paintings and drawings; the stuff that is merely good, I give to grandparents. The surplus gets thrown out when no one is looking. But I always kiss a discard first, the way a reverent person would kiss a Bible that has been dropped on the floor. That makes me feel better about throwing away sacred art objects.

I hesitate to mention it, but there is one procedure I've developed that strikes at the heart of the problem of toy accumulation. It is a summer game I call Toy Roulette. It's played with a lawnmower and the rules are simple—anything on the grass that is small enough to run over is fair game and once it's been cut to ribbons you get to throw it into the trash. It's best played without spectators.

One cold December night, just before going to bed, I went into Marie's room to make sure she was properly blanketed. In the darkness I tripped noisily over a toy truck and stepped down hard on something unyielding that jabbed the instep of my bare foot. I don't know what it was. It was pointy like Barbie's breasts, but there was only one of it. Maybe a Confederate infantryman with fixed bayonet. I gasped and sat down on the bed to feel for a wound or blood.

Marie didn't move. She lay there, breathing rhythmically, probably dreaming of more toys. Toys as big as Clydesdale horses that, when disassembled or broken, would fill our house with their thousands of malevolent parts, the way mashed-up planets turn into deadly asteroid belts millions of miles in diameter.

Something stirred in my own mind. I half remembered hearing somewhere that in a particular culture in the Orient (Java or Burma or someplace like that), each child gets only one toy: one child—one toy. A beautiful concept. Could we try that in this country? I guess we'd need a Constitutional amendment and there'd be some economic repercussions, but it just might work. I got up and left the room, sending each foot ahead like a minesweeper, excitedly wondering whether I should wake Betsy up and tell her my idea.

13. Tenth month

The baby, due in March, would move into the small bedroom currently occupied by Marie. Marie, in turn, would move into a larger room. Although our home was built about thirty years after Texas won independence, Marie's room-to-be looked as though it had been lifted whole right out of the Alamo.

The walls hadn't been painted for generations, as if impoverished priests had roomed there, polishing their humility to a high luster. The cracked plaster of the walls and ceiling seemed to offer mute testimony to the prolonged fire of Mexican siege artillery. The nicked and chopped woodwork looked like it had felt the bite of bayonets and sabers in combat-hardened hands.

We wanted Marie to develop an appreciation of Americana, but we didn't want her childhood to be played out in a setting more appropriate for the death throes of Jim Bowie.

Also, Marie would have cause enough to resent the little interloper without feeling that the baby was pushing her into the low-rent district, too. So what time I had off from work was spent spackling and sanding and painting in a frantic race with the stork.

But there was precious little time because I'd gotten a new job. I had been No. 2 editor of a fair-size weekly newspaper for a few years with no immediate shot at becoming No. 1. Now I was to be the editor of a succession of brand-new weeklies, which I would help start up, one at a time. Instead of forty-five hours a week, I was now putting in sixty. The first new office was ten miles farther from home and the next one would be twenty miles farther. The workload, pressures, and aggravation levels were much greater. The pay was exactly the same.

Betsy, though oppressed by my long, daily absences and nervous about the upcoming birth, was impressed by my progress at work. She could hardly wait to see what my next move would be.

Getting the room finished on time was the least of my worries though. I was desperately afraid of the birth experience. Marie's birth remained a vivid memory. Fourteen hours of undrugged labor. Every couple of minutes someone twisted a fork in the Betsy voodoo doll and she gasped in agony. In the later stages, I saw things that I never knew existed in the natural world.

When I was a teenager, I asked my stepmother why boys have to pick up the tab on dates. "Because women have the babies," she responded simply. I'd expected a longer answer.

Her reply neatly bypassed that ancient business in the Garden of Eden, but it seemed to make more sense in 1968, which is when our Q&A took place. The pain of childbirth as punishment for Eve's sin was fine for biblical times when there was nowhere to go. But with the advent of movie theaters, bowling alleys, roller rinks, and amusement parks, the male-female contract had to be renegotiated.

As a youth, I didn't have much use for my step-mother's theory. I was looking for a more immediate payback on venture capital laid out for hamburgers and movies. Like maybe that evening. And in a coin more appealing than the production of a screaming infant.

But on that eventful December 3–4, Betsy squared accounts not only for her own entertainments, but for the expensive pleasures of dozens of girls and women whom she'd never even met. It hardly seemed fair to put her through it again. (A couple of years later Marie would observe that women ought to be allowed to marry women so that, for the sake of fairness, they could take turns having the babies.)

Doctors generally want mothers who have already given birth via cesarean section to rely on surgery for all future babies. But Betsy was determined to give vaginal childbirth another try, so she engaged a mid-wife named Wendy to run interference between herself and the surgeons. When I met Wendy she asked me, "Do you have any fears concerning this birth?"

"How do you mean?" I asked cautiously, sensing a trick question.

"How do you feel about this birth? Is there anything you are feeling anxiety about?" she asked gently.

"You mean like fear that Betsy will die or the

baby will be choked by its umbilical cord? That kind of thing?"

Yes, that was the kind of thing she meant, and I told her I fear all those things and others that I didn't want to name because saying the words might magically make them happen.

Out in the parking lot I asked Betsy what did Wendy mean by asking if I had any fears. To me it was like asking an unwilling participant in a game of Russian roulette: "Does this make you nervous?"

"She wants to know where you're coming from," Betsy said. "She's trying to figure out how you'll behave when the moment comes and the surgeons are pressing you, man-to-man, for the signal to cut. She meant the question just the way you took it, and now she knows what she'll have to contend with."

About a month before the baby was due, Betsy was informed that it was rightsideup in the womb, which is bad. To avoid a dangerous feet-first delivery or another cesarean, Betsy went to a doctor in Allentown, Pennsylvania, who specializes in turning fetuses upsidedown. Even though Betsy took the precaution of wearing her lucky purple underdrawers, we were scared something would go wrong.

I had expected the doctor would invert the baby by reaching in and rummaging around, so I was alarmed when I saw the size of his hands. They were like baseball mitts. But as it turned out, they were perfect for the task. The doctor greased up my wife's belly and put those giant hands on it and kind of squooshed the baby around. It didn't seem very medical or difficult and it only took about a minute. Have you ever extracted the end of a drawstring that had been accidently pulled into a sweatshirt? Well, the procedure was about half as hard as that, although you probably shouldn't try it yourself in case there's a trick to it.

The due date was only weeks away when another strange thing happened. The doctors decided to extend Betsy's pregnancy by one week. Maybe Wendy had decided I needed an extra week of anxiety to strengthen my character and applied to a panel of physicians, who then voted on it. But however it came about, they postponed the due date one week.

The extension was bad news for my wife, as you can imagine. As in so many cases this was an unwanted pregnancy. The baby was wanted though, so we had to see it through.

Those final days were tough. Betsy would sleep fretfully on her side while our prenatal gymnast clambered around inside her rib cage like a rabid hamster in an exercise wheel. Every morning I would wake up and whip back the covers on the off-chance that maybe there'd be a dear little baby nestled in between us. I would have chided, "But dear, you should have awakened me." But no, there was only my long-suffering wife, coiled there like an anaconda trying to digest a whole donkey.

I did manage to finish the room, though. Hours before the first genuine contraction, the final coat of paint had been applied to the patched, scarred, and humped adobe of Marie's new room and her new bed had been set up in it. Marie, happy in her much-touted new room and feeling womanly in her "big-girl bed," would be able to meet the newcomer with the casual confidence of an alligator wrestler facing a newt.

14. The birth

There's a New Jersey legend about a woman whose labor was so brief and intense that she gave birth in a hospital elevator on the way up to the maternity ward. "Oh, I'm so embarrassed!" she told an attending nurse, once the excitement had subsided.

"Don't feel bad," the nurse replied. "Two years ago, a woman had her baby right out there on the front lawn!"

The patient moaned in despair, "That was me."

True story? All I can say for sure is that if my wife could get it all over with so quickly, she'd not only endure the embarrassment but she'd let you off at your floor, too.

On the night of April 9, several days after the new due date, Betsy was having some kind of womb situation—light contractions about ten minutes apart. The next morning we called her parents to come and get Marie. That evening the contractions ceased twenty-four hours after they'd begun. For most of the night Betsy wept with anxiety and disappointment. The next morning they brought Marie back.

Three days later at about three a.m. the sleeping giant really began to awaken, though Betsy was courteous enough to let me sleep until seven. My ever-helpful in-laws came and collected Marie again. At two p.m. Betsy said, "It's time" and we got into the car.

Normally this is a very special time for husbands. We get to drive as fast as we want and, as long as we don't crash into anything or run anyone off the road, society smiles approvingly. Glad at last to be doing something, I helped Betsy into the passenger seat and then got behind the wheel. We took off, rushing through the streets whose speed limit, for everyone but us, was twenty-five miles per hour.

I was more than half hoping that a cop would pull us over, walk over ready to enforce the law, see Betsy's condition, grin excitedly and shout: "Follow me!" He would then lead a gallant race through the countryside on our holy mission. With manly determination and skill I would wring every available rpm out of our wornout Datsun, keeping pace with our police escort, plunging forward at speeds of up to eighty or ninety mph. The patrol car's emergency lights would be whirling and flashing and, I hoped, his siren would be wailing. Anyone with any sense of style would agree with me that this is the best way to take a woman-in-labor to the hospital.

But Betsy ruined it for me. We hadn't even hit those rollercoaster hills through the farmland when she demanded: "Slow down! There's no rush and every bump hurts like anything."

Then a contraction seized her and she ordered: "Stop the car!" I obeyed, wondering if the baby would be born in the frontseat of our rusty sedan. It would not; Betsy explained that with the car in motion during a contraction "It's just too many things going on at once." So we made four stops on the twenty-minute drive.

When we arrived, the contractions were coming only about four miles apart, but the doctor was unimpressed. Dilation was only one centimeter and we were sent home. I'm not exactly sure what was only dilated one centimeter, but I knew from before that whatever it is, it has to be opened to a yawning ten centimeters before it's time to eject the baby. Last time Betsy only got to six and then gave up.

The stop-and-go drive home was discouraging, but some progress was being made; now Betsy was yelling during the contractions. Then followed a few long hours in our kitchen and at eight p.m. we made another halting drive to the hospital. This was the real thing, but after many hours of torment, Betsy was only able to dilate to seven centimeters. It beat her personal best by one, but even so, it did not qualify her for the final push. At four a.m., when her labor began to subside, Betsy, her midwife, and I all agreed it was time for major surgery.

Two hours later I was tenderly holding nine pounds, thirteen ounces, of red, crying baby. Sally. Conscious this time, Betsy smiled happily from the operating table as, for the second time in three years, the doctors and nurses sorted out the vital organs from packing materials.

Betsy's smile was beyond my understanding. She had even been smiling serenely when she'd looked down and seen what looked like a purple giant being pulled by the head from her very guts. Am I a poor sport because such a sight would make me want to scream with terror for a day or two?

And in a related matter, Betsy later expressed satisfaction that she had given an exhaustive try to vaginal birth, even though it hadn't worked out. It's great that she could come away with positive feelings. If she hadn't put that spin on the circumstances, I'd have said that Mother Nature had played her for a chump, putting her through needless weeks of uncertainty and fear capped by a twenty-four-hour festival of pain, only to go under the knife anyhow.

I haven't taken any surveys, but this could be a male/female attitude difference. Betsy, along with the best of womankind, sees pregnancy as a time of nurturing and togetherness. She sees labor and delivery as a time for the full expression of her "feminismo," which is as different from machismo as women are different from men. Although enormously painful, it is a dramatic and meaningful process, culminating in the life-giving moment of birth. A noble ordeal with the baby as the priceless prize. I respect and admire this outlook, but I don't share it.

Let me tell you how guys see things. Some of us see pregnancy as no big deal and believe that its unpleasant aspects should be just laughed off. Others of us, myself included, see pregnancy as a grotesque condition in which an aggressive and dangerous creature is actually living and growing inside another human being, squashing and pummeling the innards of the host organism and causing all the medical and emotional side effects you'd expect under such unwholesome circumstances. Then comes childbirth, a hair-raising struggle in which the human body runs amok, racked and propelled by unseen and untested clockworks that only kick in during labor and delivery, and, not surprisingly, sometimes only some of it works. But while all these spooky, iffy, loosely scheduled dilations, secretions, and contractions are going on, two precious human lives hang in the balance. The baby is a prize all right, but it's one that's been snatched from the hellions guarding the heart of darkness. To put it plainly: Men don't like childbirth.

Women wonder with justified anger and bitterness why their obstetricians, most of whom are men, do so many cesarean sections as hubby cheers them on. I'm clearly not qualified to discuss the medical reasons for performing cesareans, but I can tell you something about guys: Most of us would like to reduce the whole weird, womanly business of childbirth to a simple mechanical procedure like changing a carburetor.

This information is presented, not to excuse men for the way they think, but to let women know just what they may be up against.

I've heard it said that if men had to have the babies, the human race would die out. I don't believe that, but I'm fairly sure you'd be seeing mighty few vaginal deliveries.

But men are not having the babies, so I received little Sally into my arms and, for a second time, I carried away the newborn treasure, leaving Betsy on the operating table, pale but triumphant.

Part 2
Marie and Sally

1. Rivals

How would Sally's big sister react to her? Would sibling wrangling be the oppressive and destructive force in our home that it was when I was growing up, the second of three boys?

I have painful and shameful memories of those days. I remember joining with my older brother, Steve, to plague Jim, the younger one. We were so bad that Mom and Dad moved him out of our communal bedroom into a sanctuary of his own. But we still found abundant opportunities to harass him. We'd taunt him, call him names, lock him in his room, leap out of his closet to startle him, and cheat him out of his nickels and dimes. (Actually I was the only one after Jim's money; Steve has never had a proper appreciation for the almighty dollar.)

Jim and I had our good times. He was three years younger than me and was a good companion for riding bikes, playing alongside the creek, and building little shelters in the woods. But for every hour of companionship we shared, he paid dearly in mental anguish. I feel terrible about this now, but as I recall, when it came to being teased, Jim was as responsive as a well-tuned sportscar. The tiniest bit of teasing would get an instant and large rise out of him, which made him an irresistible target.

I don't suppose it needs to be said that our treatment of him was cruel and—just ask him—unforgivable.

Steve, two years my senior, was always bigger,

smarter, and more athletic. He still is. When we were little, my mom used to bathe us together and when we were older my dad bought us little wooden training rifles and drilled us ("Attention! Parade rest! Right-shoulder arms! Left shoulder arms! etc.). Once, in an adventurous mood in a swimming pool, Steve and I touched tongues under water.

In moments similarly intimate, we used to have sword fights. These would occur when we'd find ourselves peeing into a shared toilet bowl, a situation which occurred more often than you'd think. The streams of urine were our swords and we'd duel with them. I was a chivalrous and tidy fencer and would never go in for the kill. But Steve answered to another code and "touché!" I'd be changing my clothes. I don't know if this kind of play is healthy or sick, but I do know that thirty years later neither one of us can urinate if anyone else is in the room.

Steve and I shared a bedroom until he was fifteen and after lights-out we'd improvise stories. Inspired by the Hardy Boys detective books, he'd take the part of the older, wiser brother Frank Hardy and I'd be the impetuous, foolish Joe Hardy and we'd make up an adventure, entirely in dialogue, as we went along. Sometimes he'd be Superman and I'd be some lesser superhero like The Flash or Aquaman.

Steve always assumed the leading role in our games. When we were very small we'd dress up in cowboy clothes and Steve would be Roy Rogers and he'd make me be Dale Evans. Later, he was Davy Crockett and I was sidekick Georgie Russell. Once he read a book about Jim Bowie and for weeks afterward I had to be Bowie's brother, who was named Rezin, but had little else to distinguish him.

When we took bubble baths together, Steve, being

bigger, got to sit in the deep end near the faucet. He felt this also gave him ownership of the bubbles and I would have to trade him my best bath toys for a few handfuls of suds.

Sometimes Steve would put me in a big box and play Radio. He'd whack the box with a stick to change stations and I'd sing or tell a story or pretend to give the news, switching back and forth with each blow. The game would continue until I got hurt by one of his station-changing smacks. For Steve my screams of pain meant the station was signing off for the day— our own little national anthem.

There was another little game called Catch Blackie, named after our neighbor's dog. In a dimly lit room, Steve would shine a flashlight beam onto the wall and I'd try to catch it. A flick of his wrist would send the bright circle (Blackie) across the room and I'd run after it. A peculiarity of this game is that it is only fun for the guy with the flashlight. For the other player, always me, it was frustration itself. I could never catch Blackie and if I ever did, my achievement would be even less tangible than the physical contact that is at the core of Tag.

Sometimes Steve wasn't content with simple domination and the odd parry-and-thrust in the bathroom. Then his attentions took a more brutal turn. We didn't have *Sesame Street* on TV in those days, so we'd watch professional wrestling and *The Three Stooges*, and Steve would create his own synthesis of the martial and comic arts, which he would practice on me. He won any scrap we got into, thanks to his greater size and coordination and his association with the likes of Moe, Larry, and Killer Kowalski. But I would take revenge in my own skulking way.

His vulnerable spot was his model airplanes. We

would buy those Aurora or Revell kits, and following the directions exactly, paint and glue them together, working many hours in front of the TV set. When the planes were done, we'd get thread and straight pins and hang them from our bedroom ceiling so they looked like they were flying. We took great pride in these planes, the way they looked and all the disciplined labor that went into them.

So whenever I lost a fight with Steve, instead of going back for a second helping of mano-a-mano punishment, I'd furtively get a razor blade from our model-building equipment, sneak up to our room, climb up on a chair, and cut down one of his airplanes. I didn't actually *cut* the threads; I'd seen enough detective shows in which a sleuth picks up two neatly sliced ends of rope and says, "This has been cut!" So I'd just scrape up and down on the threads so it would look like they had been worn out by natural causes. Though what those natural causes could be in our bedroom, I couldn't imagine. Motes of dust bashing against the threads wearing through them over a period of a few months? Thread fatigue? A mystery.

I'd usually pick a plane that was over a hard surface like a desk or a bedpost, so it would sustain maximum harm when it hit. Sometimes, when I wasn't satisfied by the damage, I'd throw the plane down a couple of times.

It only takes five kills to qualify as an ace and I won that distinction easily. Over the years, I downed a Japanese Zero bomber, a U.S. Phantom jet (this one was hardly worth the cutting; very sleek, few parts sticking out to break on impact), an English Spad World War I biplane (I got that one twice, a year apart), Charles Lindbergh's "Spirit of St. Louis," and the Wright Brothers' Kitty Hawk original (this one crash-landed in such a mess of struts and rigging that I was almost sorry).

I never brought down more than one of his aircraft every other month and he never seemed to wonder why his planes always bit the dust and mine never did. Smart as he was, he never figured out that the little brother he used to thrash so routinely was making hash of his air force.

Our childhood home certainly wasn't devoid of fellowship and fun. But it also contained much unnecessary cruelty and destruction of which my parents were only partly aware. I hoped that Betsy and I could do better.

Sally was only twenty-four hours old when, excited and nervous, I brought our three-and-a-half-year-old to the hospital to meet her sister. Marie was delighted to see the ruddy ten-pounder and smiled broadly at her. She gave the baby a little fuzzy, gray bunny she'd gotten for Easter. (She reclaimed it a few minutes later when it became apparent that the baby was not going to play with it.)

Marie beamed with pride and pleasure when we sat her in the center of the bed and put Sally into her lap for some gentle petting. Then it was my turn to hold the baby. I picked her up and suddenly Marie had to have a drink of water. "In a minute," I said. "I'm holding the baby right now."

Did you ever wonder how the Indians felt when it dawned on them that the palefaces weren't just visiting North America for a few weeks of fresh air and religious freedom? Marie looked up at the Great White Father holding the much-heralded baby, and suddenly the downside of the deal hit her like a ton of buffalo chips.

Dressed in one of the hospital's little blue sterile

gowns, Marie announced darkly, "Nobody will ever pay attention to me!" and stalked into the closet.

She was muttering to herself, but her words were muffled by bathrobes and street clothes. Still holding the baby, I hunkered down by the closet door to hear what she was saying. I could only catch stray words like "never" and "nothing." Oh no, here we go, I thought. Twenty years of just what I deserve.

Betsy let Marie sulk for a while and then said some magic words that brought her out of the closet like a shot. In a loud voice Betsy exclaimed, "Oh look, there's a little bit of poop on the baby's blanket." Marie rushed out almost breathless to see the almost indiscernible speck. I had reckoned without my wife's genius for child distraction.

Peace was reestablished, but we didn't kid ourselves—like the Indian's, Marie's way of life would never be the same and from time to time there were bound to be uprisings.

2. Cousin Heather

On a mild sunny Sunday in May, Marie and I sat on the front porch of her playhouse. I was thinking about maybe resuming the great unfinished work of my life— the job of painting our real house. Marie was busying herself with a new set of little, white, plastic dishes that would never look the same again.

She made a stew of mud and grass and dished some up. "C'mere Daddy. Drink some soup." I felt pretty good; it looked as though Marie and I were about to relive the previous summer, which really had been pretty wonderful. But time plunges ahead for parents and kids. Before the day was out, some little kids from the neighborhood, including Marie's cousin Heather, had added our yard to their orbit and Marie to their gang. In the course of just one afternoon Marie moved up to a new plane of existence. She was now a neighborhood kid.

Although there still was time for us to play games of make-believe and to discuss life over a cup of mud, much of the time I was now a mere observer to the goings-on in our yard.

Cousin Heather, daughter of Betsy's sister Susan, was an impish four-year-old. The family had moved in a block away from us during the winter. At family gatherings Heather had always seemed somewhat okay, but once she got used to us, she let her hair down.

This new uninhibited Heather liked to walk into our house without knocking (in clear violation of the Bill of Rights), and once inside she would order a little snack from Aunt Betsy or me, whom she regarded as scandalously unresponsive servants.

But Marie was Heather's main target. Besides telling her all manner of scary tales about predatory birds, monsters, and devils, she was chronically incompatible with Marie. They never wanted to play the same game and Heather would attempt to resolve their differences by haranguing Marie with vigor and at length.

It seemed like every time I'd check on them, I'd see Heather, hands on hips, leaning toward Marie, showering her with abuse. And poor Marie would be looking at the ground, shamefaced. It was a delicate situation. My first impulse was to run over, grab the malignant little imp's ponytail in one hand and the seat of her pants with the other, and throw her in the direction of her home. (She couldn't have weighed more than forty pounds and I bet I could have heaved her twenty feet or so.)

But that wouldn't do. There was Aunt Susan to consider and besides, Marie might come to count on that service every time she found herself with a little interpersonal problem.

We considered forbidding Marie to play with Heather. Tempting, but rejected as overbearing, over-protective, and likely to cause trouble within the extended family circle. I suggested we have a heart-to-heart with Heather's mom, but Betsy said that, as a child, Susan had been just like Heather and probably was proud that the little pill had turned out so true to the original.

Ideally, Marie should either identify Heather as an annoying creep and discard her or learn to deal with her domineering personality. It's not easy to remodel a destructive relationship, but we gave it a try.

We let Marie continue to associate with Heather, but with one new rule. The kids could not play at Heather's house. They had to play in our yard or in our house. This was so that Betsy or I could monitor what Heather was saying to Marie so we could help Marie understand when Heather was out of line and then privately supply her with the verbal ammunition needed to turn back Heather's assaults on her self-esteem. Also, at Heather's house, Marie might have a problem reconciling the concept of "company manners" with the social rough-and-tumble she'd need to handle Heather.

This worked pretty well. One afternoon, after Heather had gone home for lunch, I sat down in the backyard with Marie to give her a pep talk about Heather's bossiness and the need for self-assertion.

It wasn't long before we heard Heather's bicycle pulling up in front of our house. Her bike seemed to suit her perfectly. Remember the brand of child's bike mentioned earlier that is painted black and named Li'l Dominator? I didn't make it up. Heather owned one. It was tiny and had training wheels on it that were worn down to the metal. Consequently the bike had a distinctive and unpleasant clanking and grinding sound that we'd hear four or five times a day, warning us of her arrival.

Anyhow, Heather dismounted and walked around into our backyard. Marie was primed and announced without preamble, "Heather, you think you're the boss of everyone. But you're the boss of no one."

A lesser foe would have stayed to argue. Not Heather; wordlessly she turned on her heel, walked back the way she'd come, and in a moment we heard the sounds of her bike in departure mode—a scuffling, clattering noise like a dozen metal rats wrestling in gravel. She gave us the rest of the day off.

Another day, Heather and Marie were in our yard. The girls were going to play House. Heather was insisting that Marie be the baby and Marie was refusing, probably because on other days Heather had reduced Marie to tears by calling her a baby. In any case, Marie was resisting that role with all her might. Finally, like a prizefighter who's had enough, Marie came over to where I was pretending to be reattaching a leg to our picnic table and explained the problem to me. "Help me stand up for myself," she urged.

"You have to do it for yourself," I told her, figuratively rubbing her shoulders and fanning her with a towel. "If Heather tries to make you do something you don't want to do, just tell her what you think about it."

"But every time I want to talk, she's already talking," Marie said. I considered lending her my hammer, but decided against it.

There was a series of ads on TV a few years ago which described a certain type of mother as "a Kool-Aid Mom"—the one "with-it" mom on the block who could be counted on to serve up an icy beaker of sugar-water to the delight of every child in the neighborhood. I'd aspired to be sort of a Kool-Aid Dad, but that ambition faded fast under Heather's influence. And when she'd come over, the only thing tall and cold around our house would be me. She and I would exchange looks of frank dislike and I'd make it a point to say no to at least 90 percent of her requests and questions.

As summer arrived, Marie's commerce with Heather diminished. With our encouragement, if Marie had anything at all to do, such as run an errand to the bank with me, she'd send Heather home. Gradually Heather's visits thinned out to where we'd only see her once a week or so.

At first I felt like a goon having an enemy who is under four feet tall and no heavier than a bag of dog chow. But I reckon I'd be a worse goon if I'd let that sharp-tongued flyweight give my little champ a bad pounding without throwing the occasional folding chair in through the ropes at her.

3. Gun control

Marie and I were gathering and stacking scraps of lumber that had been lying on the ground near the garage. I think we were pretending to be Donald Duck's nephews piling up library books, but we could have been Hansel and Gretel finding slices of bread. Sally was snoozing nearby in the stroller and Betsy, trowel in hand, was herding some azaleas around the yard.

Suddenly a five-year-old boy in camouflage fatigues charged into the yard clacking away at us with a pint-sized replica of an automatic assault rifle. Billy.

We liked Billy. Apart from his murderous impulses and games of terror and menace, he was a goodhearted kid and when he played with Marie he showed traces of kindness and respect. But we did not like to see him in combat regalia, playing at war crimes, especially because of his influence on Marie.

Marie's requests for armaments had been denied, except for a pair of bright-blue water pistols which had been approved by the narrowest of margins by the House Subcommittee on Murder and Mayhem.

Billy was disappointed that his attack had neither felled us to die in agony nor sent us fleeing for our lives. He received two adult frowns and Marie's mild interest. Luckily for Billy he hadn't awakened Sally, or there might have been real bloodshed. Marie said, "Hi, Billy," and put a stubby 2-by-4 onto a pile.

"Hey Marie!" Billy said, "let's play Army. You can use my bayonet."

That sounded like something I didn't want to see, so instead I brought out the water pistols and set up a bucket of water. Billy gladly put down his black and olive-drab plastic accouterments and the kids spent a half hour chasing each other around the yard happily getting soaked.

I suppose it still qualified as gunplay, but I didn't want guns to turn into hugely desirable forbidden fruit. Besides, the gaudy blue pistols didn't really seem to be the stuff of which gruesome and sadistic fantasies are spun.

And I ought to know. In my youth I was as gun crazy as anyone and I didn't get over it until about ten years ago.

When did this fixation begin? I have a 1955 photo of my brother Steve and myself, dressed in Davy Crockett suits with vinyl fringe, coonskin caps on our heads, and powder horns hanging from our necks. But no rifles. My unfashionably avant-garde mom had forbidden her boys to have guns.

But the restriction proved to be unenforceable. My mom soon learned that Steve and I were beating up smaller kids in order to steal their cap-guns. Mom preferred her boys to be make-believe assassins rather than real ones and the ban was lifted. However, the damage to our tender psyches had been done. My brother and I spent the next twenty years as gun enthusiasts.

Although Mom still drew the line at BB guns, Steve and I built up an arsenal of cap-guns of the Colonial, Civil War, Wild West, and World War II eras. We also had dart guns and water guns.

We even invented a rubber-band gun out of Tinker Toys that could fire up to five rubber bands at once. I'd outline the principles of it here for the amusement of children on a rainy day, but this weapon was rendered obsolete by a much handier and more accurate machine gun invented by my pal Eddie Meier in 1960, which consisted of clothespins nailed to a flat board.

Of course the single-shot gun remained unbeatable for accuracy when held in the hands of an expert. This was nothing more than a foot-long ruler with a rubber band hooked over the top edge and held in place with a forefinger. I spent whole days sitting on the playroom floor, watching Westerns on TV and firing rubber bands at a collection of toy soldiers and plastic animals. If I had spent that amount of time throwing a baseball around the yard, my name would be a household word today.

But one day in 1963 the pleasure faded. While I was engaged in this peculiar pastime, my parents were watching the TV coverage of the assassination and funeral of President Kennedy. My dad remarked with disgust that Lee Harvey Oswald probably had spent his boyhood shooting rubberbands, too, and my little sport suddenly lost much of its appeal. Lyndon Johnson had barely led his dawgs into the White House when I had already refocused my energies on blowing up my old model airplanes with firecrackers.

Nevertheless, when I went to Boy Scout camp a year later, I spent every spare minute at the rifle range firing .22s. In college I was captain of our dorm's intramural rifle team and when I graduated and went West to whoop it up for a couple years in the state of Washington, the first thing I did was buy a secondhand revolver for shooting bottles and cans.

My big brother's love of guns was being indulged at the taxpayers' expense in the U.S. Army. While Steve was mastering the .45 automatic pistol and the M16 rifle and generally helping to make the world safe for McDonald's, my preoccupation took a strangely sentimental turn.

I decided I ought to buy a cowboy-style six-shooter intending that it should become a family heirloom. After some research and a visit to every gun store and pawnshop in Seattle and Tacoma, I finally bought an expensive Swiss-made revolver with rosewood grips and brass fittings. In my mind's ear I could hear wee voices clamoring, "Grandpa, show us the gun you got when you lived Out West!"

But as with most boys, my passion for firearms finally disappeared. It was knocked down by the onslaught of common sense and smashed flat by the weight of responsibility. And when Marie was born, it was replaced by a much less colorful, but much more powerful obsession—child safety. As soon as she learned to walk, I gave my gun collection a farewell oiling and put it away indefinitely in the attic of a childless friend.

And if I ever think of my handsome Swiss .357 magnum, I imagine the voice of my as-yet-faceless son-in-law telling his wife: "Marie, if that old coot tries to show his rusty six-gun to the kids again, I swear I'll put him in a home!" Which sounds reasonable to me.

But meanwhile Marie's man of the hour was showing a more openminded attitude toward guns. Dripping water and brandishing a fistful of blue plastic, Billy was besieging Marie's playhouse. Squirting valiantly out of a side window, Marie yelled happily, "Stay outta my fort or I'll kill you!" I guess she didn't mean anything by it.

4. Bad words

The next day Marie's fort had reverted to a house, but the scene was not much more peaceful. She was inside it with Heather, who was leaning out the window scolding Billy. Marie had explained to me earlier that because Heather and Billy don't like each other, when they play House, Heather and Billy are the mommy and daddy, but they are divorced. Marie is their child who sometimes lives in the playhouse with Heather and sometimes in the garage with Billy.

I was in the driveway leaning into the engine compartment of one of our miserable heaps, trying to loosen the oil filter. The wrench slipped and I gouged my knuckles on something sharp-edged and greasy. I'm not a spontaneous person, but for the moment all inhibitions vanished and I gasped the F-word as I dropped the wrench. Withdrawing from under the hood, I hit my head on its underside and happened to kick over a bucket of dirty motor oil.

As the pain subsided, I became aware of a three-year-old presence behind me and turned to find Marie a few feet away, her eyes as big as headlights.

I sat down on the ground, partly to be closer to her and partly because the Earth's gravitational pull seemed to be a little stronger than it had a minute before. It wasn't until Marie had offered to kiss my grimy and bleeding hand and gotten a full explanation of why I'd injured it, that she remembered why she'd come looking for me. To tattle.

"Daddy, Heather called Robbie an ———." It was a vulgar term for a well-known bodily orifice.

When I was growing up, a kid who said a word

like that could expect to be marched into the bathroom to have his mouth washed out with soap. (To this day, I can't smell Ivory soap without remembering the taste and tenor of those emotionally supercharged scenes of crime and punishment.) And thus we learned an important lesson.

The lesson was: Don't use foul language unless you want to get a big reaction. Adults universally agreed that bad words were a big deal, so they became a big deal. I can't exactly say why I use such words in moments of sudden pain, but it has something to do with the magic and power with which those words were imbued in my childhood. No matter how much feeling a child put into the word "ouch," it could never make an adult turn purple and swoop upon you like a starving condor.

I remember at age nine, sitting in a neighborhood sandbox with a few contemporaries, holding a whispered discussion on what word was absolutely the dirtiest. One boy nominated the F-word and others favored the S-word. Both words were brand-new to me, but the consensus in the box was resoundingly for the F-word, even though no one seemed to know what it meant.

A couple years later my expanded vocabulary paid off. I was in the backyard with my frail little brother Jim. We had one of those snow sleds that are shaped like a contact lens, made of aluminum and measuring about three feet across. I was passing time by heaving it into the air as far up as it would go, like a huge Frisbee. It wasn't going very high—only high enough for Jim to wander under it. It struck him a stunning blow on the head. He fell to the turf and for half a minute he was too stunned even to cry.

Of course my heart went out to my little brother

in his moment of misfortune. That's what it was—a misfortune. An accidental twist of fate. But I had a bad record for being the catalyst for these twists and I knew that would count against me in the Court of Mom.

Jim soon exploded into sobs and screams of "I'm telling Mommy!" As he staggered to his feet, I suddenly knew what to do.

"Wait a minute!" I said, gently restraining him. As persuasively as possible, I said, "Jim, if you don't tell, I'll teach you the dirtiest word in the entire English language."

He hesitated and then he was mine. "Okay," he said. Really he wouldn't be giving up much. The odds were that he'd have something else almost as bad to report to Mom within twenty-four hours.

"But first, you have to promise that you'll never ever say this word," I said, realizing I could beat this sled-throwing rap only to be brought up on charges of corrupting the morals of a child.

He agreed and I taught him the dreaded F-word. "What's it mean?" he asked.

"I don't know," I said, "but it's very dirty."

Jim was not a satisfied customer. He felt like I'd sold him an empty bag—a four letter word, delivered incomplete, without a definition, and even if he could find out what it meant, he had promised not to use it. But a deal was a deal and besides he was all calmed down by now and if he did go tattling to Mom, his testimony, delivered without tears and sobs, would be entirely unconvincing.

I like to think that such a transaction would never take place between my daughters, partly because bad words are easier to come by nowadays (Marie could've learned a nice juicy one from her old man that afternoon if she hadn't been so distracted by the visual part of the incident) and partly because my wife and I have agreed to underreact to bad language.

So when Marie used her dirty word, I said casually, "I guess you know that's not a nice word to say. Right?"

"I know," said Marie, "but I'm only saying what Heather said." (Only three and she'd already mastered that fine point of schoolyard law—that quoting a curse word is nowhere near as bad as using one afresh. Luckily she couldn't cite the landmark case which helped establish this principle—Ben Franklin Elementary School vs. Ricky Epstein, 1961.)

And that was the end of it, for the time being anyway.

When I was a kid, saying dirty words was considered immoral. It was in a class with assault, theft, and cruelty to animals. Although in our house we aim to make it merely a matter of etiquette, I'm not eager to hear from Marie other particulars of the ugly domestic give-and-take between Heather and her "ex," nor do I feel it's time yet to release Jim from his promise.

And if Marie is paying closer attention the next time a sudden turn of events draws involuntary expletives from my lips, rather than try to explain why her dad would say rude words, I might try to downplay the outburst by telling her that these are automotive-repair terms, which is true. In our driveway anyhow.

5. Bored

"I've got nothing to do," said Marie with the forlorn air of a space traveler who is a few years into an indefinite stay on a desert planet devoid of other life forms, weather, electricity, books, or board games.

The fact is, Billy and his little sister Jennifer had just been called home for lunch a minute earlier, leaving Marie suddenly and instantly bored. So Marie had come into the kitchen to see if I would entertain her.

"Let's eat," I suggested. Marie sat on the kitchen counter while I cooked some hot dogs.

"What are their names?" Marie asked as I put two dogs into a pan.

"Frank and Edweena," I replied. The animated-food game was part of our lunchtime routine and it rolled along comfortably with a script that was unwritten but unvarying:

"Pertend they don't like to be in the pan," she prompts with a trollish glint in her eye.

I comply with falsetto complaints about the heat and lamentations about an unpromising future, which continue until they are delivered into nice, cool buns and their burns are treated with mustard. "Ah, that feels good," sighs Frank. Edweena, the hot dog that I'll be eating, has fallen silent, leaving Frank to express the feelings of both.

"I *like* you, Frank," says Marie, picking up dog and bun. She then points to one end of the hot dog and whispers to me: "Pertend this is his feet." This distinction is made by Marie to ensure that her first bite does not take in Frank's speaking end, thus snuffing out the dialogue at its most poignant juncture.

As her teeth sever Frank's lowermost 10 percent, the script calls for a cry of pain, loss, and betrayal. "Ow! I thought you said you like me!? You shouldn't bite someone you like."

Marie then spells it out for poor Frank: "I do like you, but you are food and I like you in an eating way." Her voice is filled with amusement mingled with sympathy. This is her big joke and its delivery marks her favorite part of our game. It's sort of the denouement. Frank has no good rejoinder and pretty soon his dying cries are muffled and finally extinguished.

Our lunchtime tragicomedy varies with the menu. There is another favorite in the series in which slices of bread are the finicky protagonists who protest when they are smeared with peanut butter and jelly. They are then outraged when they are stuck together. But their problems are finally put into perspective by the flashing teeth of my lovely daughter.

One time Marie was given a couple of talkative cookies for dessert. After the first one was eaten, the second one refused to go anywhere near Marie's mouth. Then Marie told it: "If you go into that cave, you'll get to meet Santa."

Betsy is faintly amused by these dramas, but has no inclination to take even a minor role. She, too, likes food in an eating way. Period. At this particular luncheon, after Frank's final cries of despair had echoed and died, and Marie was capping him off with a milk chaser, Betsy changed the subject: "How was that libel seminar at work Friday?"

"Boring," I replied.

Marie put down her glass and looked at me in astonishment, her eyes wide. "I thought *nothing* was boring to grownups!" she said.

That made sense. Occasionally you could coax an adult into having some fun, but generally they like their hot dogs unnamed and unspeaking and their entertainments as bland as their lunches. To a little kid, a grownup complaining of boredom is like a fish complaining of humidity. Grownups seem to exist in a sea of boredom, but not only do they endure it, it seems to sustain them. More than a few minutes out of it, say in a roughhouse romp on the lawn, leaves Dad prostrate and gasping, trying to wriggle back into his home element. Like a whale after ten minutes of touch football.

Grownups talk about things like mortgages, car repairs, money, politics. (And God help the child who tries to interrupt one of these conversations to say something *interesting!*) We read books without pictures. We watch news, soap operas, and baseball on TV. At the beach we lie motionless on the sand. Plus, we think clothing is an ideal gift to give or receive.

To a child, the unbearable tragedy of all this is that adults have the money and power to make every day an orgy of delight. It breaks a child's heart to think of the toys that could be purchased with an adult's paycheck! On any given Saturday, parents could take their kids to a zoo, circus, or amusement park. But the sad fact is that they are more likely to spend their Saturdays trying to sleep late, reading newspapers, writing checks, and doing laundry. To most kids, their parents are like those recluse millionaires who dress in rags and die of starvation. What a waste.

Worse yet, parents try to inflict their anti-fun feelings on their kids. Thus a running child is warned, "You'll get overheated." A joyously whooping child is told, "Calm down." A child about to dive into a chocolate cake is warned, "Take a small piece; that cake is too rich." A child who gets a cash gift of more than twenty-five dollars is informed, "This goes into the bank for college." Although grownups never forbid children to have "too much fun" in those exact words, that is their obvious aim. You know those safety badges that are worn by workers in nuclear plants? The chemically sensitized badges that turn purple when they've soaked up too much radiation? It's as if every child wears an invisible Fun Badge that his parents monitor to be sure Junior hasn't been exposed to unsafe levels of fun.

While grownups are actively pursuing it, boredom is childhood's bane. Like hemophilia to the royal families of Europe.

I can remember it well. In fifth grade I used to pass the time in class by figuring out how old I was in days, then in hours, then minutes. On days when I was feeling less cerebral, but just as bored, I would make a list that started with the time school let out. It would look something like this:

2:30
2:29
2:28
2:27 . . .

and so on, right down to the moment of list-making. Sometimes, if I got bored early enough in the day, the list would cover several hours. Then I would watch the clock and put a check mark by each minute, once it had been endured. (I still do this at long wedding ceremonies with printed programs, ticking off each song, speech, and sermon as soon as it is accomplished.

Betsy disapproves of this, but someday they'll skip something and everyone will be glad I was keeping track.) My fifth-grade checklist never was a very smart technique for making time pass. It pretty well stopped it dead.

And, as near as I can figure it, a child's perception of time is a major contributing factor to boredom. If a dog year is seven human years, a child year is more than twice that. So when Dad clicks off the flow of morning cartoons, the ten-minute lag-time before Junior finds something else to do, leaves a bleak, yawning gap in her life that stretches ahead like a life sentence in solitary confinement.

Another contributing factor is a child's lack of obligations. Look at it this way: When a grownup knows that he should be preparing his income-tax return, painting the house, reading a trade journal, and mowing the lawn, there is nothing going on in the perceptible world that won't become enormously fascinating and absorbing. Also, it's hard to be harried and bored at the same time.

But just when I think I've figured out kids' terrible susceptibility to boredom, I'll find Marie contentedly watching a videotape of *Charlotte's Web* for the fourteenth time, or I'll observe her playing all by herself, peeling the wrappers off her crayons, murmuring, "C'mon Blue, let Yellow try on your clothes. Are you cold? You can snuggle here next to Purple, okay?"

It makes me feel like a surgeon who confidently sews up the patient and then discovers a couple of important-looking organs lying under the operating table.

6. Questions

A late-summer storm had blown a few shingles off the roof of the playhouse, so I was up there nailing on some new ones. Betsy and Baby Sally were in the house and Marie was standing on the ground looking up at me. "Daddy, can invisible people see each other?"

Good question. Marie and I had run up against some invisible people in one of the Oz books a couple of weeks before, and I guess Marie was still thinking about them. I rested my hammer against the peak of the roof and scratched my head. It was a tough one, but I could handle it. "No," I said thoughtfully, "they can't see each other."

"Oh," said Marie, absorbing the information. With that matter cleared up, she shifted gears and proposed that we pretend that she was Br'er Rabbit and I was Br'er Fox hiding up on Br'er Rabbit's roof. Ten minutes later I had given up roofing and was chasing her in circles around the playhouse as she laughed and taunted, "Can't catch me, Br'er Fox!"

Ever since Marie could talk, she'd been asking questions. Some of them, especially at first, were the automatic how-come questions, which are like slugs dropped into the conversational jukebox. They are aimed more at generating some sounds at minimal mental expense than at trying to learn something.

But by the time she was closing in on her fourth birthday, most of Marie's questions were pretty good. One day, playing with a feather-duster, she asked, "Are these real feathers?"

I told her yes and she asked, "What kind of bird are they from?"

"An ostrich," I said with casual expertise, covertly reading the handle.

Squeezing the plump core of the feather-duster, Marie asked with bright interest, "Is there ostrich meat inside here?"

One day she and I were driving down the highway and Marie was gazing up into the sky, lost in thought. Finally she said, "Mommy, where would clouds take you?"

I explained to her that I'm Daddy and that clouds are thin like fog and if you sat on one you'd fall right through. She took this in stride but I immediately regretted my answer. One minute I'd been the father of a child who believed that you could go for a ride on a cloud and the next minute I was not the father of such a child. I felt like I'd actually grabbed one of her ankles and yanked her down out of the sky.

Other misapprehensions I don't mind setting straight. One night while gnawing away at some spare ribs, Marie asked with mild curiosity, "Are spare ribs from people?"

"No, they're from pigs," Betsy told her.

"Pigs!?" Marie cried in dismay. "Somebody killed a pig?!"

And speaking of meat, another day there was a groundhog in the street in front of our house. It was panting and flies were clustered around a wound in the back of its neck.

Marie questioned me about the animal and I told her I thought it was dying. A down-to-earth neighbor, an amiable excavator named Mr. Hartpence, waited until I'd taken Marie indoors before he took a shovel off the side of his dump truck and confirmed my prognosis with a merciful blow.

That night, thinking about the events of the day,

Marie asked soberly, "Daddy, do all animals and people die?"

"Yes."

"How about people's stuff, like houses and toys, do they die too?"

I wish my answers were as good as her questions. But who could match wits with someone capable of wondering, "What's under Mickey Mouse's skin?"

But sometimes I try. One weekday morning Marie asked, "Daddy, when you go to work, do you do the same work every day?"

"No," I answered, "Some days I'm a policeman, some days I'm a cowboy and the rest of the time I'm a dog doctor."

"Really?!" she asked, on the verge of new respect for her old man.

"No, I'm only kidding," I said. "I do the same thing every day." (Although my enthusiasm and effectiveness vary.)

Marie doesn't mind getting a silly answer on the first try, because she knows that a followup reality check will always get her the straight skinny. That kind of playful, but ultimately trustworthy, service is the best I can offer to a child and I've done my best to adhere to that policy without fail.

September came and with the opening of pre-school, Marie began a new line of questions that apparently reflected the curriculum. "What is the sun made of?" (I don't know, but it's on fire.) "Does Cousin Elisabeth (a Norwegian) live on another planet?" (No.) "Does the sun have any other planets?" (Yes.) "Why don't we fall off the Earth?" (Because we're on top of it.)

I'd hoped that Marie's questions wouldn't take this technical turn until she was seven or so. I knew that soon I could no longer pass myself off as the ultimate source of wisdom and fact and, like fathers of big kids everywhere, I'd be pathetically reduced to offering mere opinion.

7. Halloween

With autumn comes the third-biggest day in Marie's calendar (after Christmas and her birthday). Marie had spent the two previous Halloweens in a tiger suit that had been made by her Grandma. We got two years' wear out of the suit because Grandma had made it big and because at age three Marie's memory was so short that she couldn't remember the tiger suit from the year before.

This year Marie had put in a bid for a Peter Pan suit and Grandma had obliged once again. The pattern she used yielded a green-felt suit that had a little more of the forest gnome to it than the more swashbuckling outfit worn by the Peter Pan we know from the Disney classic. Marie's outfit consisted of green tights, a tunic that was cut jagged at the bottom so as to suggest leaf-tips, and a leaflike hat and shoe covers.

At the risk of overthinking something that doesn't require much thought, I must say that Betsy and I were pleased by Marie's choice in costumes. Marie has a disturbing tendency toward pessimism and playing games in which she is a target of scorn, derision, or even physical abuse. For example she likes to take the role of Rudolph the Reindeer and then asks me to be one of the other reindeer who "used to laugh and call him names." And don't forget the sick ducks.

Tigers, though sometimes vicious, are lively, bold, and strong. Peter Pan is cheerful, aggressive, and full of himself. He's also irresponsible and boastful, but Marie has no inclination toward those problems. It makes me wonder if kids pick Halloween identities that reflect qualities they possess or qualities they lack.

Of course you have to exclude from consideration any costume that is thrust upon a child as a matter of convenience. Sally is plainly destined for tigerhood, and I remember an ugly yellow-and-blue clown suit that materialized in my boyhood home and was inflicted upon whichever hapless brother was the right size for it that year.

But I'd bet that a psychologist would find out a lot by asking his couchant patients about their Halloween alter egos.

"Well, Doc, let me see. I've been a clown, a chickie, Davy Crockett—"

"Yes, you mentioned the Davy Crockett costume at a previous session, Mr. Epstein. You had no gun, as I recall."

"That's right, Doc. My mom made me a frontier-type outfit when I was four. It was wonderful, but it really needed a rifle and she wouldn't let me have one."

"And how did that make you feel, Mr. Epstein?"

"Inadequate, Doctor."

"Now we're getting somewhere. What other costumes did your mother make for you?"

"I remember a red suit with a pointed tail. It had a hood with black horns sewn onto it."

"Your mother dressed you up as the devil?"

"It wasn't like that, Doc. I was just *a* devil, not *the* devil. My mom was a Lutheran and didn't think much about Satan. My brothers and I were being raised Unitarian and, never mind the devil, we just barely had God."

"Okay, Mr. Epstein, tell me some other costumes you wore."

"When I was about eight, my mom dressed me up as a girl for the Cub Scout Halloween contest. I wore a beret, a blouse that buttoned the wrong way, and a skirt. I can't remember what we did about my hair. Anyhow, I won second prize in the girl category and my mom said I was very pretty. She said my rosy complexion was wasted on a boy. . . ."

I daresay each of us could unlock a similarly crammed attic full of emotional furniture to a trusted therapist.

But the selection of a developmentally beneficial costume is not a parent's only worry. The Halloween season is an overflowing cornucopia of danger. There's something to fear for every parent. Parents of big kids can worry about Mischief Night. Parents of medium-sized kids can worry about pedestrian safety and dangerous strangers. And parents of little kids can worry about sugar overload.

It's one of life's mercies that new parents are dealt the mildest of the problems. With Marie and Sally aged only four and one, we'd have several years before they'd want to go out trick-or-treating unchaperoned. Likewise our neighbors would have several years before flaming paper bags of dog poop—a staple of Mischief Night hijinks—began appearing on their doorsteps, courtesy of the Epstein girls.

Mischief Night is observed unevenly across the nation, but here in New Jersey it is recognized by youngsters as the night before Halloween. It is the core of a mischief season that, sooner or later, gives every child who is old enough to go out after dark a chance to define his own moral code.

In my youth the scale of mischief began with the harmless sprinkling of dried corn kernels on doorsteps. At the time, I didn't see how the corn-scattering was any kind of mischief at all. Looking back, I suppose the resident, upon discovering the kernels on his stoop in the morning, would feel somewhat violated. But this was too subtle for me and I rejected the practice as some kind of wholesome substitute for mischief.

At the other end of the spectrum was real vandalism. Some kids would throw rocks through windows and bend car aerials. Somewhat less wicked were the pumpkin-smashers.

I found my mischief in the middle range. My specialty was car-window soaping, with the occasional furtive ringing of a doorbell. I once lit a smoke bomb on a neighbor's porch and another time I threw a raw egg at a stranger's storm door. But I wasn't comfortable with these acts and, like a weak swimmer, hurried back to the shallows.

On Mischief Night, 1960, my big brother and I soaped "Nixon" onto the windows of every car in our neighborhood. I was nine years old. Our next-door neighbor, Al Hirsh, went around soaping "Kennedy." I don't think we changed anyone's mind but all three of us felt really good, having hit upon a harmonious blend of mischief and civic involvement that is hard to achieve outside of elected office.

But the dilemma presented this Halloween was of a nutritional nature. How to maintain our ban on candy while encouraging Marie to enjoy everything else that Halloween has to offer. Although the rule was laid down by Betsy for reasons of health and behavior, I cherish the notion that the kids, deprived of a preoccupation with candy, may channel their enthusiasm toward things of the mind and spirit—for example, focusing on the costumes, fantasy, and pageantry of Halloween. Dreamer or hypocrite, I'll admit that as a kid, candy was my alpha and omega.

Betsy rose to the challenge. She took Marie trick-or-treating to the homes of our friends. But first, like a shrewd commodities broker, Betsy bought up Marie's candy futures with a new box of sixty-four crayons.

When the time came to deliver her harvest, Marie showed signs of reneging. But my wife is hard to surprise. From out of nowhere she produced a deluxe Peter Pan coloring book to sweeten the deal. The candy was willingly surrendered and everybody was happy. Especially me; I got to dispose of the contraband. Halloween was still the season that tests my moral fiber. Who would have figured that a teenager could resist smashing pumpkins only to become an adult who would take candy from a baby?

8. Carefree

We have an old picture book called *The Little Red Caboose*. And in it there's a panorama of a freight train going through a village and here and there are people, pets, and farm animals watching it go by. Whenever I read it to Marie, I am struck by one detail of that picture—a little boy standing at trackside waving at the train.

That boy is less than a half inch tall on paper, but whenever I see him, a wave of self-pity washes over me and I want to cry. (Then comes a wave of self-disgust and my equilibrium is reestablished.) Generally, the boy reminds me of my own departed youth; more specifically it is the boy's carefree air that gets me. If I were to imagine a life for this kid, it might contain problems—a little harassment by the class bully, a few low marks in Spelling or Penmanship, that kind of thing—but kids can live in the present and I can tell that this kid, even though he's so small on the page that I can barely count his eyes, hasn't got anything on his mind except that it's a Saturday and maybe the brakeman in the caboose will wave back to him. I can't see much of his wrist, but I know he's not wearing a watch.

It's not that I do a lot; it's just that I realize what all I should be doing. I know I'm neglecting my family for my job but at the same time I feel I really ought to be spending more time at work. At home, besides feeling I should be at work, I feel that I ought to be minding the kids, visiting my old dad, cleaning out the attic and garage, replacing cracked windowpanes, doing yard work, or painting the rotting trim on our house. The fact is, apart from doing the acceptable minimum on my job and some light child care, I don't get around to doing much beyond feeling the weight of all the things I should be doing.

In November, when I broke away from my responsibilities for the Third Annual Guys-Only Weekend, I had that little, picture-book boy in the back of my mind. Betsy had been generous about releasing me for another long weekend in St. Petersburg. But I knew that five days and four nights of single-parenting would challenge her mental toughness all the more rigorously because while she was crawling around the floor looking for Marie's shoes, and bleary-eyed at three a.m. changing Sally's diaper, I'd be as unencumbered as a cat.

Marie had something to say on the matter. After reading some of *The Wizard of Oz* one night, she asked: "Why does Dorothy live with her aunt and uncle? Where are her mommy and daddy?"

"Dead, I guess," was my unadorned reply.

"No, I think they went to Florida," Marie said, without smiling.

Since the previous year, Russ had moved down to St. Pete and this time, instead of crowding into Tommy's apartment, we stayed at Russ's house. Doug and I arrived late at night and went to our beds after only an hour or two of talking with Russ and Tommy. The next thing I knew it was morning! It had been my first undisturbed night of sleep in months, maybe years. I was refreshed and pleased, but still I felt strange—as if I'd missed something. Like someone receiving a head wound at Pearl Harbor and waking up in 1950.

A good night's sleep was important because Russ, our vigorous social director, ran our holiday like a children's camp. Reveille was at nine, followed by a well-planned morning activity, an afternoon on the beach, and an evening activity. I don't especially like being on the beach, but the others seemed to crave it and our beach time there did make a good buffer of inactivity between each day's entertainments.

On the afternoon of my first day there I sent a postcard to my brother: "Dear Jim, Florida is wonderful. I've decided to relocate here. If you see Betsy and the kids, give them my regards." Just a joke of course, although my psychological advisers insist that there is no such thing. Which may be why I felt guilty about the joke.

That evening before leaving for the greyhound racetrack, I dutifully scrounged up change, found a pay phone, and called home to check in with my loved ones. Marie missed me but was coping. Betsy missed me but was likewise coping (with Marie and Sally). The baby hadn't noticed I was gone. To be honest, I missed my wife and kids about as much as I missed my dad during my first wild, drunken Saturday night as a freshman at Syracuse University.

But the next morning, at the Seminole Cultural Center and Gator-Wrestling Arena I took great pleasure in buying Marie an Indian headdress and a necklace consisting of a fake bear-claw on a leather thong and sending her an alligator postcard, supposedly from Al the Alligator, telling Marie he'd met her daddy in Florida and had been encouraged to send her this picture of himself.

Later that second day, we were putting in our mandatory afternoon beach time when an odd little ballgame started up. One of the guys would pitch a yellow-green tennis ball to another guy who would bat it with the metal handle from the beach umbrella. The other two guys would be in the outfield chatting. No score was being kept and no particular prowess was being exhibited or looked for. Positions would be traded whenever anyone felt like it. It wasn't big fun. It was relaxing and almost boring, but we seemed to have all the time in the world. Our involvement in such an idle pursuit seemed to prove it. I had ceased being glad to be away from my family and was just about to miss them. Even guilt had disappeared. I had attained my moment of weightlessness, a moment that lasted for an hour or two. I was that boy in the picture book.

That night when I phoned home our answering machine picked up. I was glad that they weren't all moping around the house, but I was disappointed.

On the third morning we rented a motor boat and went out into the bay. We saw a few dolphins that I would have loved to show Marie and I found my thoughts turning to Betsy and the kids in the fondest way. That afternoon on the beach I found myself trying to divert the conversation from JFK assassination theories to my own accounts of cute and clever things my children say and do. And I found myself trying to interest the guys in photos of my children when there were perfectly acceptable bathing beauties well within ogling distance. I knew what I was doing, but I couldn't stop myself.

The nightly telephone call again put me in touch with the answering machine which seemed to be bearing up well in my absence.

The next day I boarded a jet bound for Newark Airport. Within twelve minutes of takeoff I managed to show my emergency photographs of my kids to the woman sitting next to me. A fearful flier, I keep a picture of each child handy just in case the pilot announces imminent doom so I can see their beloved faces one more time. (Though I suppose no pilot would make such an announcement as it would only invite panic and last-minute criticism.) But we cheated death with a safe landing and I was soon fighting my way through New Jersey traffic toward home.

I bounded up the front steps, gifts in hand, ready to sweep Marie up in my arms for hugs and kisses. When I came in the front door and hollered, "I'm home!" Marie came hopping out of the bathroom, pants around her ankles and a streamer of toilet paper in her hand. Affection had to yield to hygiene, for the moment anyway.

That night, long after lights were out and the appropriate marital rites had been performed, Marie appeared at our bedside like a wraith, saying sadly, "I'm lonely." I carried her back to her own bed. "Will you snuggle with me?" she asked, and I lay down beside her and we both fell asleep. Her wiggling woke me up later on and I retreated to my own bed.

Then the baby woke up crying. I went in and rediapered her and presented her to Betsy for milking. I dozed off despite the commotion beside me—wild grunting and thrashing and cries of "Ouch!" and "Hey, come back here!"

It was still dark when I awakened again. Sally had been re-filed in the cage-bed, but a little spook had materialized at bedside again, moaning "I'm lonely." I hauled her into the sack. I was glad to be back, but I knew I would miss those short Florida nights.

Looking back on that weekend away, I see it as an exercise centered on the achievement of a carefree state. The first part of the weekend I was burdened by the idea that I would have to return to my responsibilities too soon and the second part of the weekend I was burdened with the idea I wouldn't get home soon enough.

I was like an artillery mortar round that is full of speed and purpose both on the way up and on the way down, but in between, at its peak, it is weightless, stationary, and pretty much just hanging out. Time stands still and you can wave at a train or play ball with some middle-aged boys.

9. Well, Virginia...

Marie looked up from a book about Rudolph the Reindeer and asked, "Daddy, is Santa real?"

The moment I'd been dreading had arrived. If I were the newspaper editor who wrote the famous "Yes, Virginia . . ." essay I would have replied, "Yes, Marie, there is a Santa Claus. He exists as certainly as love and generosity and devotion exist." But I know Marie well enough to be sure that she wanted fact, not philosophy. She wanted to know if Santa Claus is a living, breathing, sweating human being and she was asking the one person she could trust for the unvarnished truth. That's our deal.

A neighbor of ours wrote a letter to the editor of our local weekly, the *Delaware Valley News*, warning parents that when your child finds out you've been lying about Santa, he might doubt some of your more important theological teachings. Everyone I've spoken to about this scoffs at the idea. They put Santa Claus (and the Easter Bunny) into a special category where the usual principles of truth and falsehood do not apply. But to me they do, and they always did.

I remember vividly an angry three-year-old standing on a curb yelling repeatedly at Santa Claus: "You fat phony!" The old gent was riding by on the last float in the gala Thanksgiving Day parade in Trenton, New Jersey. Mothers covered their children's ears and moved them away.

It is my earliest recollection—hollering up at Santa. I remember my thoughts and feelings perfectly. I wasn't trying to say that this particular Santa was an imposter. I was trying to say that there was no Santa

Claus at all and I was outraged that the whole adult world was conspiring to make me believe a lie.

I have no idea where my disbelief came from. I lived in a Santa-believing household. My Lutheran mom led the way and both my brothers followed happily.

That irate iconoclast of 1954 has grown up to be a troubled part of the Santa conspiracy. Here is the extent of my complicity: Besides unrelentingly basting Marie in Santa lore and generally talking up the magical elements of Christmas, I have made sure that the gifts that were allegedly from the North Pole were wrapped in paper unlike the wrapping paper on the gifts from Mom & Dad. I have encouraged Marie to leave out carrots for the reindeer and cookies and milk for Santa. In the dead of night, after assembling a tricycle, I have eaten those carrots and thrown the stubs out toward the tiny house where the reindeer would have paused. Then I poured the milk back into the carton and ate the cookies, leaving the plate and milky glass on the kitchen table. (Since dirty dishes are not an arrestingly unusual sight on our table, I grind about half a cookie into stagey-looking crumbs and, for a more dramatic effect, lay the glass on its side, as if it had been left in haste—by someone who was expected at every household in Christendom before dawn.)

It is wrong to perpetrate these deceptions, but it would be even more wrong to rob little Marie of the excitement that comes with believing that her gifts were manufactured by merry elves instead of underpaid Asians. (Though to give myself credit for buying American, the Roadmaster trike was punched, cast, and boxed in the Midwest.)

A few stories and a little flimsy circumstantial evidence, such as carrot stubs on the back porch, are all it takes to keep Marie convinced. My wife believed in Santa clear into the third grade on the strength of an aural hallucination she'd experienced years earlier— she swears she'd heard the clatter of tiny hooves on the rooftop.

Lots of kids extend their believing years by refusing to scrutinize the Santa story too hard for fear the line of supply from the North Pole would collapse under the weight of analytical thought. They are like buyers of stolen goods willing to accept the explanation that the items fell off a truck. Others, even more cynical, flat-out pretend to believe, like mission hoboes yelling insincere amens for a meal and a bed.

Although I am capable of fraud, I couldn't lie to Marie's face any more than I could disillusion her. So when she asked if Santa is real I said solemnly, "I can't tell you. You'll have to decide for yourself."

"C'mon, *really*," she pressed with a quizzical smile. She'd expected a joke, a fact, an opinion or, at worst, an "I don't know." But even her followup question drew the same peculiar non-reply.

Since then I've also treated questions about the Easter Bunny and the Tooth Fairy the same way. I have taken a harsher line on Disney World though. Marie had the impression that it was a real place where Donald Duck and Mickey Mouse resided and everything looked like somebody drew it and that camera crews went there and filmed cartoons on location. Because we aren't going there until Sally is old enough to stand in line for an hour, I figured that Marie would be able to wait more patiently if she knew that we are holding her back from a mere amusement park, not a genuine otherworld experience.

With regard to my no-comment stance on Santa, I can't help but wonder if my virtuous posturing and gutless word-mincing will turn out to be worth the trouble. My wife understands my big moral dilemma and thinks it is about as significant as a wrestling match between ants. "Look," she told me in the privacy of our boudoir, "if you think you can raise Marie in such a way that she'll grow up and have nothing to tell her psychiatrist about you, guess again, pal."

She's right. On the couch, children are like industrious traffic cops: If you're not reckless or drunk, they'll always be able to cite you for a dead taillight or bald tires.

10. Misconceptions

I never believed in Santa Claus, but I believed almost anything else. My mom told me that if you went-to-the-bathroom in the woods, the rabbits and skunks would find and desecrate *your* home for revenge. I didn't see how they could figure out where I lived. They weren't about to follow me home in broad daylight. Maybe they could do it by scent. I didn't know— science can't explain everything, especially when you're seven years old.

My dad had me believing another woodland whopper. He said that one day my mom was walking in the woods and it got very cold, so the squirrels gave her their fur to keep her warm and that's how Mom got her gray squirrel fur coat. I like to think I was extremely young when I fell for this one, but even in my gullibility I had problems with the squirrel story. Wasn't the fur attached? And even if the squirrels could get it off, how could a coat be assembled out in the woods without sewing equipment? What held the story together for me was the belief that my mom would never be cruel enough to send a few dozen cute, innocent squirrels to their deaths just to have a nice coat.

I also believed there were three sure ways to die: touch a light switch with wet hands, sustain any kind of blow to your temple, or eat an entire tube of toothpaste.

Everyone grows up with his own changing set of misconceptions. Most of them seem to spring from misunderstood or misleading remarks made by grownups. But not all of them.

On New Year's Day I made a list of four-year-old Marie's current array of misconceptions:

- That watching lots of television is an effective remedy for most illnesses.
- That there really are twelve days of Christmas and although we celebrate only one, families with more fun-loving parents observe all of them.
- That if you put a broken rubberband under your pillow, the Rubberband Fairy will give you a nickel for it. (This was Betsy's contribution to the world of the supernatural. Marie's playmate Nyssa believes in the Scab Fairy, someone you don't want rummaging around under your pillow, no matter how much she's paying per crust.)
- That the main thing my wife likes about me is that I always eat everything on my plate.
- That the whole business of time and clocks is a lot of bogus mumbo jumbo that grownups invoke whenever they want to make a child go to bed or get dressed and they don't have a *real* reason to put forward.
- That Tom is the mouse and Jerry is the cat.

(And she will calmly but implacably argue the point for as long as you want to pursue it. She also is sure that Babe, Paul Bunyan's blue ox, is named Dave.)

• That you shouldn't drink water right out of the river because fish pee in it. (When I caught her sipping the impure waters of the Delaware, I was too rattled to tell her that the fish are the victims, not the offenders. Many towns along the Delaware discharge inadequately processed sewage into the river, and although herring, shad, and other species seem to be thriving in it, that's not to say that they feel really good about themselves.)

• That it's normal for a woman to keep her wedding bouquet in the glove compartment of her car. (As noted earlier, this represents Betsy's compliance with the laws of inertia. After a couple years of forgetting to take it out and store it somewhere, the glove compartment became its place.)

• That the terms "idiot" and "stupid" are off limits to children until they become old enough to drive.

• That a dog would make a good housepet. (Who knows where she ever heard of such an impractical and unhygienic arrangement?)

Sally, just barely a year old, couldn't talk, so I had to exert my powers of intuition to catalogue her misconceptions. Consequently some of them I was more sure of than others. Here they are:

• That anything you can't put in your mouth cannot be fully experienced or enjoyed.

• That mother's milk and babyfood are mere basics that must be supplemented by intensive foraging on the floor. These low-lying foodstuffs range in palatability from dust bunnies on the low end to crumbs of Play-doh, a special delicacy. (She could be under unblinking surveillance on a freshly scrubbed floor and suddenly she'd be working her mouth like she was about to lean out the window of a pickup truck and let fly. A probing adult finger would find anything from a short crayon to a piece of tree bark.)

• That it is a cruel fate that has given her only two teeth and put them side-by-side instead of in opposition to each other.

• That standing up in her highchair is essential to the digestive process.

• That full nutritional value can be derived from babyfood by smearing it directly onto the skin. (It also has a pleasing visual effect.)

• That any attempt to wipe her mouth or nose is degrading and insulting and must not be tolerated.

• That toilet-training is necessary only for people who plan to go into certain high-profile lines of work, such as retail sales or public relations.

• That because people are always poking her tummy, pinching her fleshy limbs, and admiring her chubbiness, she is being raised as a meat animal.

Of course as her conversational skills developed, I was able to disabuse her of some of these misconceptions and teach her some more worthwhile new ones. (Naturally, I don't want her eating up our toothpaste and polluting the forests.)

11. The missing moms

It was the first fairly warm Sunday of spring, a beautiful crocus-coaxing March day of 65 degrees. Marie and I rounded up a couple of blankets, a stack of kids' books and a bag of pretzels and went out to the tiny house to enjoy some fresh air and old stories.

We snuggled in the blankets and I read to her abridged picture book versions of *Heidi*, *Pinocchio*, and *Bambi*. We'd just opened *Peter Pan* when the backdoor of the big house opened and Sally toddled out unsteadily and stood reeling at the top of the steep porch steps like a drunk about to be sobered up the hard way. Before I could disentangle myself from the blankets to save her, Betsy popped out, matter-of-factly grabbed Sally by the back of her overalls, and casually lugged her back into the house.

Marie and I looked at each other and shrugged. After we'd settled down and found our place in *Peter Pan*, it dawned on me that nobody in any of these books seemed to have a mother. Heidi's was dead. Pinocchio had been handcrafted by his celibate dad. Bambi's was shot by hunters. And Peter Pan had allegedly run away from his mother the day he was born.

Not wanting to upset Marie, I kept my thoughts to myself. Later on, when Marie got up and began gathering last fall's leaves, twigs, and other materials to make herself a giant bird's nest to sit in beside the playhouse, I considered my discovery further and, taking out my little notebook, compiled a list of well-known motherless protagonists:

Tom Sawyer, Huck Finn, Cinderella, Snow White,

Hansel and Gretel, David Copperfield, Oliver Twist, Luke Skywalker, Orphan Annie (duh), Dorothy Gale of Kansas, The Little Mermaid, Beauty (and the Beast, too, for all I know), Tom Swift, the Hardy Boys, Nancy Drew, Pippi Longstocking, Hoss Cartwright, Mickey Mouse, Donald Duck, and the rest of the early Disney characters.

You can add to that list just about anyone ever portrayed by Shirley Temple. Betsy can't stand Shirley Temple movies. She says the child makes her gag and certainly no one, especially impressionable little girls, should watch more than three Shirley Temple movies a year. But I think that what really disturbs Betsy is the mortality rate among Shirley's screen mothers.

Besides the orphaned Heidi, there is *Susannah of the Mounties* (mom killed by Indians), *Curly Top* and *Bright Eyes* (by motor vehicle accident), *Captain January* (by shipwreck), and *Stowaway* (by Chinese rebels).

So why all the missing moms in literature? Because since the beginning of time, good mothers have been conscientiously keeping things from happening. So the best writers, from the Brothers Grimm to Mark Twain, know that if you want things to get really out of hand, subtract the mom and the rest is as easy as casting an orphan into a dungeon.

Occasionally a writer will try it backwards. Louisa May Alcott kept mom with the kids and sent dad off to fight the Civil War. And if you've read *Little Women*, you know Miss Alcott bet on the wrong horse. While dad is off fighting for his life and the Union, the reader is stuck home with mom making dresses and listening to piano recitals.

It is literarily okay to let a dad stick around. Fathers just aren't the bulwark against disaster that mothers are. In fact, a dad, left alone with a child or two, can be counted upon to move the story forward by marrying the first witch who applies.

At first blush, *Jack and the Beanstalk* seems to discount my theory about moms. It's Jack's dad who is dead and mom is right there, vigilant and aggressively sensible. In fact she even helps out by throwing the magic beans out the window in disgust, effectively sowing the seeds for Act II. But what would have happened if mom had gone with Jack to sell the family cow? No beans, no stalk, no giant, no story. Just a routine, rustic, cash transaction that wouldn't even have merited a back-page mention in even the most scrupulously complete storybook.

But to really examine the mom factor, turn to Edgar Rice Burroughs, author of the Tarzan series. He had more trouble with mothers than any writer I know. When Tarzan of the Apes is still a baby, Burroughs kills off his folks, Lord and Lady Greystoke. It was a grim necessity: Burroughs had to clear the way for a foster parent who would give the baby an upbringing proper to a budding apeman. And sure enough, a female ape adopts the lad. Whoops, another mom. So Burroughs has her done away with, too. Speared, I believe. Thus the avenue to adventure is reopened.

But before too many volumes in this twenty-two-book series have elapsed, the mom problem resurfaces. Jane, who had done wonders for the plot when she was a fainting, blushing coquette from Baltimore, soon becomes a mom of the worst wet-blanket sort. By volume four, *Son of Tarzan*, she and Tarzan are living in London and their teenage son, Jack, hasn't even been told that his dad was ever anything but a British nobleman. That's because uptight Jane has forbidden any talk of her husband's past. But Burroughs makes quick work of this—he gets the lad away from the stifling influence of his mother by having him shanghaied to Africa. Seventy pages into the book, young Jack is making a name for himself on the Dark Continent as Korak the Killer, swinging from branch to branch, slaying wild beasts and beating up on men of all sorts—pretty much doing business at his dad's old stand.

That's not the end of it, though. Tarzan and Jane move back to Africa and whenever Jane gets to be too much of a mom, Burroughs has her kidnapped and sometimes she's missing for whole books at a time while Tarzan searches for her in a halfhearted and poky manner, taking time out along the way for meals and naps and World War I.

(In the first version of one of the stories, as it was published in a magazine, Jane is killed by German soldiers. My brother Steve, who knows more about the Tarzan books than anyone else on his block, tells me that Burroughs's own mother was disturbed by this and gave Edgar a talking-to. And when the story appeared in book form, lo and behold, Jane is not killed but only kidnapped. It seems that Burroughs's mother-trouble straddled the world he created and the one he had been born into.)

Like Burroughs, Dr. Seuss, in his magnum opus, had to get the story out from under mom. But since he believed that kids get enough of murder and abduction from the fairytale classics, he gets rid of mom simply and humanely by just sending her out shopping. Thus her home and children are left vulnerable to the vandalism and terror of a raid by the Cat in the Hat. (If mom had been at home, the Cat would have been marched straight to the vet to be "fixed," hat or no hat.)

The first flush of pride at my discovery slowly

faded into resentment that fathers seem to be held in such casual regard. Marie was wallowing around in her nest, sharing her body warmth with a brood of croquet balls she'd found and adopted. I considered getting up out of the blankets and doing some meaning-ful, fatherly yard work, but then decided that I had done enough for one Sunday. Before long the afternoon warmth was waning and it was time for Marie and me to take the croquet balls inside.

12. Sickness

There's nothing quite so frightening as trying to com-fort a baby who's burning up with fever, or rushing into an emergency room at four a.m. carrying a tot who can't breathe. Due to a lung situation that we hope she'll grow out of, Marie has afforded us these special moments. The doctors call it variously bronchi-tis, pneumonia, allergies, and asthma, but whenever Marie catches cold, an infection causes the passages in her lungs to swell and close. Then she is gasping for breath, her lungs whistling and wheezing, and her little body racked by fits of desperate coughing. This takes place a few times each year, usually during the winter.

The first times it happened, it seemed to me she would die. She was so hot and her lungs sounded like nothing I'd ever heard before, except maybe the distant and jumbled honking of a flock of Canada geese. Her hold on life, at these times, seems so fragile and chancy. For temporary relief Betsy or I wrap her in a blanket and carry her outside to breathe the cold night air. Or we fill the bathroom with steam and take her inside although this scares her.

But she has survived a lot of rough nights and bounced back from many bouts of illness and all indications are that she'll continue to do so. The wonder drugs that pull her through are two kinds of medicine. Marie calls them the Good Red and the Bad Pink.

I have tasted them and the only way you'd think the red was good is if you've had the pink. The red medicine is almost as thin as water. It kicks her lungs open and also elevates her mood and makes her run around like a maniac. The pink medicine, which is thick and disgusting, is an antibiotic that kills the infection that is at the root of the problem.

Marie doesn't mind the red stuff, but the pink makes her gag. At first, to get her to take the pink I tried the old "Oh yum! It's cherry flavored." Marie found this highly offensive—partly because of the obnoxious inaccuracy regarding yumminess and partly because I was denying her due credit for braving the awful stuff. Yes, the flavor is cherry, but a cruel, mockery of cherry. Metallic, as if it had been extracted somehow from the cherries in a casino slot machine.

Marie will take the medicine, but she'll make it into a fifteen-minute procedure—a thirteen-minute prelude of yawning and coughing and trying to beg off, then two minutes of attacking the teaspoon in series of little forays with drinks of water in between. With each sip of medicine she shudders with revulsion and makes a face that gives the impression that she is trying to put physical distance between her mouth and the rest of her being.

That April Marie closed out the season with a sudden decline into illness, but this time Betsy was away in the Caribbean. After gamely seeing me skip off on three annual guys' weekends, Betsy had finally gotten a chance to miss her family—five days in Jamaica with Pete and Mary, a hip couple who have made the island their second home and go there a few times a year. They avoid the tourist traps and make their stays in parts that are remote, peaceful, and cheap.

I would take care of Marie and Sally with the help of my in-laws, our twelve-year-old babysitter and— as it turned out—our pediatrician. The first day went pretty well. I even took a nap while the babysitter took the kids to the park. But on the second day, Marie caught cold and started coughing and inside of twelve hours she was gasping for breath in the throes of lung congestion. That night she was unable to sleep and in the daytime she could only cry and moan. Even television couldn't distract her from her misery. While trying to comfort Marie, I kept one-year-old Sally busy by feeding her Cheerios, one at a time in a constant flow all day.

A low point came after we'd gone to the doctor and were in the pharmacy waiting for prescriptions for the red and the pink to be filled. I held Sally. Because the aisles are so narrow it was impossible to keep her out of grabbing distance of the merchandise I had to keep moving and whirling her around so she couldn't get a fix on the grab-ables. Meanwhile, Marie had made a little nest out of her coat and lay down on the floor, exhausted from a sleepless night and weak from her illness.

Another low point came that night when Marie, nauseated by the repulsive pink medicine, vomited it (plus plenty of liquids) all over her bed and, with tears in my eyes, I had to make her take another dose of it. No sooner had Marie dropped into uneasy sleep, than poor Sally, whom I'd been neglecting for days, woke up crying. I changed her diaper and sat holding her in the rocking chair easing her back to sleep while Marie wheezed and coughed in the next room.

In the darkness I pictured Betsy in the tropics, at that moment certainly sleeping soundly, her body slowly processing the exotic mixed drinks of the day before and resting up for another busy day of sunbathing, lolling, and basking. I would wait and see what the morning would bring. Maybe Marie would respond to her awful medicine or maybe I'd go out and find the kids a wicked stepmother.

13. Babysitters

Walking behind the eighth-grade babysitter as she went through the gloom of a February dusk from the car into our house, I felt an urge to call her back and, there on the front walk, to say in a low-key, almost confidential way:

"Uh Jennifer, I don't want to make you nervous, but it's vital that you know that Marie and Sally are the two most important creatures on the face of the earth. Your good report-card, your stylish clothes, your cute boyfriends, all are as dust and ashes compared to the happiness and well-being of these two glittering treasures. Guard them with your life." But it might make her nervous and I couldn't afford to frighten her off or we'd be stuck at home, guarding those glittering treasures ourselves.

Parents with little children are in an unfortunate

position on the population charts nowadays. They are on top of one hump and their kids are on top of another hump. The valley in between explains the shortage of teenage babysitters.

In the face of these demographics, a friend of ours took drastic measures. She got hold of the junior high yearbook and looked through it with her little daughter, catalogue-shopping for a babysitter. Our friend sought faces that showed compassion, resourcefulness, courage, honesty, sobriety, and chastity. Her child looked for a twinkle in the eye and a kind smile on the lips. But when they were approached, the most likely teenagers proved to be either uninterested or unavailable and by the end of this exercise in human resources, the mom was ready to hire any youngster who didn't look plainly dangerous.

I know another hard-pressed mother who always leaves her babysitter well supplied with ice cream, snack cakes, and candy on the theory that she'll lose a Saturday-night babysitter if the girl gets down to a slinky dating weight. Hard times make hard people.

If only all the responsible teenagers of babysitting age would make themselves available, the situation wouldn't be so bad. Part of the problem is the wages. A babysitter usually gets the same rate of pay for presiding over a peacefully sleeping household as she does for an afternoon of backyard riot duty. Industrywide reform is called for. Because a fair wage scale would attract more teens into the personnel pool, I have sketched the outlines of just such a system.

The base rate would only be two dollars an hour, plus one dollar for each additional child. When the kids are asleep, the rate would revert to the basic two dollars. But few parents would be charged the base rate; neighborhood babysitters' councils would evaluate your children and assign them a personal-charm and behavior rating (A, AA or AAA). They would also rate your household on amenities, such as MTV, snacks, heating or air-conditioning, and a good VCR movie library. A low rating would cost you a babysitter–hardship surcharge; however, a triple-A rating would get you a discount.

Thus the parents of two angelic children who live in a well-appointed home would get price breaks that could have them paying as little as two dollars an hour, while the parents of bratty kids in a home devoid of cable TV and Diet Coke could be paying as much as six dollars an hour. When my system comes into general use, it will do for babysitting what the photocopier has done for office humor.

Once we increase the numbers of available babysitters, we can afford to get particular about their habits and attitudes. I did a lot of babysitting in my youth. I did a fairly good job, but looking back, I am appalled by my casual approach to a huge responsibility. As the occasion demanded, I fed them, diapered them, drew pictures for them, read to them, or spanked them, never even dreaming of the tragedies that I was there to avert.

Twenty-five years later, I have a much more fertile imagination. When we leave our two precious daughters in the care of a largely unknown teenager for the evening, I manage to block the possibilities out of my mind for most of the time. But driving home, my more negative side takes over. If the evening's entertainment has turned out to be less fun than we'd hoped, I'll remark to Betsy, "I'll never forgive myself if anything has happened to the kids while we were at *that* movie."

But even after a wonderful night out, the closer we get to home, the more pressing my fears become.

Nearing our street I look for ambulances and fire engines. Until our house comes into view I'm half expecting to find only a smoldering pit of charred timbers; or to find it surrounded by a tangle of parked cars while inside rages a rock 'n' roll riot of sex, drugs, and breaking glass, with our shellshocked children cowering under a bed. When the house is in sight, if any lights show in the upstairs windows, I think of sudden illness—food poisoning or maybe a burst appendix.

But so far we've found nothing amiss. (Although one morning I noticed the name of our favorite babysitter inside a heart had been spray-painted on a concrete wall across the street from our house. The babysitter lives across town and I wonder what business her swain might have lurking around over here. But maybe I worry too much. The graffiti valentine could be addressed to some other Urania.)

After a night out, I wait in the car to take the babysitter home and Betsy goes inside to resume command. When the groggy babysitter stumbles into the car, I pay her fee and, with my unsaid cautionary remarks firmly in mind, I ask pointedly, "Are both the children alive?" (This question brings new babysitters wide awake.) Upon hearing an affirmative answer, I peel off another dollar bill and say, "Good work. Here's a bonus."

I'm slightly embarrassed to perform this little debriefing routine, but I force myself. When I used to babysit, I had no idea why I was there. I want these babysitters to know why exactly.

14. On the job

New Jersey drivers are not quite as reckless as Boston's nor as rude as New York's, but in terms of numbers and spirit, I'd say we are not far behind. A real Jersey driver has a rule and an attitude: He never gives an inch and he sees all other motorists as his mortal enemies.

One afternoon about twelve years ago I was negotiating a massive jam near Flemington when I outmaneuvered and thus offended a man driving an old white station wagon. A bad sport, he honked angrily from behind me and in the rearview mirror I saw his wife shake her fist.

Obeying basic rules of the road, I rolled down my window and gestured appropriately. To my embarrassment, a shift in the traffic put the station wagon right beside me a second later and the woman passenger, infuriated beyond sense, flung open her door and was getting out to come and attack me physically.

But before she was fully on her feet, she realized that she was holding a baby against her shoulder and subsided back into the car. Once I saw that she wasn't going to claw my eyes out, I looked straight ahead, praying for a break in traffic. I felt something wet on my arm and turned to see the woman pointing a baby bottle at me as if it were a flamethrower. Then the traffic parted and our shared moment ended.

At the time, red-faced, I was only thankful that the woman hadn't been breast-feeding. But now that I'm a parent too, my thoughts run deeper and I understand better how difficult it is to separate the parental role from the other aspects of your life—whether you are an irate passenger anxious to discipline a skillful (though possibly discourteous) driver, or whether you are a lowly copy editor of a mid-size daily newspaper, which was the job I landed in early spring.

Work and home have complementary effects. Each place has a wearing effect, but the wear occurs on different surfaces of my soul and psyche. So leaving home to go to the office, or leaving the office to go home, is like rotating a car's tires. It prolongs the usefulness of the unit without actually giving it a break.

Even though it takes an hour to drive from our home in Frenchtown to the newspaper office in New Brunswick, I'm unable to make a complete transition from family mode to job mode. In my early days at *The Home News*, mealtime was the most difficult. Eating in the company cafeteria, usually with a few co-workers, I'd find myself looking frequently and critically at their plates to see if they were doing good jobs on their dinners.

And if one of them should gesticulate in my direction to emphasize a conversational point, I would quickly fade back by reflex, fearful that the darting hand would grab my good clothes in a slobber-and-food-smeared fist and impair my look for the day.

I'd eat fast, too, because in the back of my mind I'd expect that fifteen minutes into the meal one or all of them would climb into my lap. So, for practical reasons, I'd want to have the main knife-and-fork action done by then.

Although children seldom appear in *The Home News* newsroom, I have a persistent feeling that they are all around me. When I hear foul language such as "shut up" or "stupid," I experience a quick surge of vexation, but I usually manage to bite back any admonition. In the heat of the moment I've been known to call someone a "silly-dilly" or to say, "Liar, liar, pants on fire!"

One day that first spring at *The Home News* I saw a paperclip on the floor and automatically stooped to pick it up so no one would choke on it. Usually, though, I behave like anyone else, except that I generally try to treat younger employees with kindness figuring that, after all, they're *somebody's* children.

This attitude is not particularly professional, but maybe the world of work would be a better place if more people carried their household sense of caring onto the job site. Think about it. For every sales rep who suffers an undeserved spanking, I bet there'd be two vice presidents saved from putting their eyes out with message spindles.

Could this wave of gentleness ever spill out onto the highways? I don't think so. Around here, when people were putting yellow warning signs in their car windows saying: "Caution, Baby on Board," some drivers saw these signs as curt demands for special consideration. Others saw them as pathetic cries for mercy. But in no instance did any of the signs ever cause anyone to give an inch.

15. Our house

Springtime was going full blast. Flowers, sunshine, robins, balmy breezes, etc. A young man's fancy might have turned to love or baseball. Mine just kind of slipped into neutral.

Marie was up the street. The last time I'd looked she and the neighborhood kids were engaged in a peculiar biking activity that they enjoy. Three to five kids ride their bikes and trikes around and around in the street in all different directions, but all staying as close as possible to each other. It's like what you'd expect from the U.S. Navy's Blue Angels precision flying team on their first day of practice. Lots of collisions and no real formation—just sort of swarming, which they somehow find satisfying despite the certainty of occasional injury.

In the frontyard Betsy was in her flower garden, digging up the dirt with a big shovel. One-year-old Sally was toddling around, effectively corralled by my fence. Getting into the spirit of the season, she'd wander over to the turned earth and quickly cram a fresh, rich handful of it into her mouth. Then she'd stick out a muddy tongue and spit and drool while Betsy excavated with a forefinger. Everything seemed to be under control here, so I went indoors for a cup of coffee.

Maybe this was the day I would resume my job of painting the exterior woodwork. Our house did need help. It was built in the 1870s and sometime between then and modern times, one corner of the kitchen had sunk six inches and other bad things had happened to its alignment. Also, the clapboard exterior had been covered with asphalt shingles and painted a dried-mustard color. When I bought the house a dozen years ago I painted about half of the wooden trim. Now that paint was peeling and the trim I hadn't painted was rotting.

Once when Betsy had a friend over for lunch I tried to make her believe that we'd just bought the house and were very excited about its potential. I had heard the word potential used so often by other people talking about our house, that it came easily to my tongue. But by the time we were brushing the crumbs off our lapels, I admitted to Betsy's friend that this house would be lucky to achieve a coat of paint and a few new windowpanes; its potential would have to wait for its next owners.

As if Betsy had somehow tuned in on the direction my thoughts had taken, she came into the kitchen. "Rick," she said (I hate it when my wife calls me "Rick." Usually she doesn't call me anything and I prefer that. When she calls me Rick, it means that whatever follows will be, in Betsy's opinion, serious or important). "Come outside and take a good look at the house. It looks like it should be in a documentary on Appalachian poverty. Can't you please do something about it?"

I never disobey a direct order. As Betsy and Sally went to harass the vegetation in the backyard, I went and stood out in the street and took a look at the house, trying to view it as a stranger might. It didn't look too bad—unless you realized that people actually live in it. Apart from the ugly color and the peeling, rotting woodwork, the house has a posture problem— the outer walls slant in just a little, the roof sags a little, and you get the subtle impression of a big upside-down W.

It's hard for me to project my kids into the future, but something about the appearance of our house sent me about five years forward. I imagined I was a fly-on-the-table in the faculty lounge at the Frenchtown Elementary School:

First teacher: "Do you know anything about Sally Epstein's home life?"

Second teacher: "Do I? Just look out the window and across the ballfields. See that yellowish-brown house? That's where she lives!"

First: "Oh, the poor dear! That explains it."

Second: "Explains what?"

First: "Explains why I caught her in the lunchroom about ten minutes ago eating a peanut-butter-and-dirt sandwich."

Second: "Say no more!"

I frowned and propelled my troubled mind another half-dozen years into the future. This time I was an amorous teenage boy, resting astride his bicycle and gazing across the ballfields at the home of the talented and desirable Epstein girls.

When I was an adolescent I felt that the otherwise-ordinary homes of pretty girls had a certain sexy look to them. I remember the appealing brick split-level where Lynn Johnson resided and the demure colonial inhabited by Carol Soule. The small, yellow-shingled house where Pat Ewan lived exuded some of her magic, its mystique teasingly enhanced by the way it was half-obscured by a billboard in the frontyard. I would walk by these houses with racing heart and peek at them as furtively and as eagerly as I would at an inadvertent display of lingerie in study hall. Not only that, but when I visit Lawrence Township and drive by these houses, they still excite me a little, though the girls who lent them enchantment are long gone.

I took a good look at our house. I imagined that in my teenage veins flowed a 50–50 mixture of red blood and fresh testosterone. I imagined that up in their rooms those Epstein girls were doing those erotic, private things that regular teenage girls would be doing up in their rooms in the twenty-first century. Writing in diaries, having pillow fights, painting their toenails, piercing each other's noses, giving each other real tattoos, and I don't know what else. But no matter how hard I tried, this did not look like a sexy-girl house. It looked like a house where an old man lets newspapers accumulate in stacks until they tower to the ceiling and lives his life in little pathways between them until one day some of the piles topple and crush him. And if he isn't half-eaten by his two dozen starving house-cats before anyone misses him, he can count himself damned lucky. You know, *that* kind of house.

Nevertheless I tried to imagine a young swain coming up to our front door to collect his date. With nervous courtesy he shakes hands with the father who then sends the little sister upstairs to tell Marie her date is here. But the images just wouldn't take hold.

I had to admit, ours looks more like the kind of house where the boy would whack the side of it with a stick and yell, "Hey! Come outta there!" And where would he take a girl from such a house—to a nice restaurant and a stage play? Out for burgers and a movie? How about into a concrete pipe with a bottle of bad wine?

This wouldn't do. No wonder Betsy had pulled me out of the kitchen to handle this façade crisis. I took a tall, wooden extension ladder out of the garage and leaned it against the front of the house. I climbed up and hung a paint can from an upper rung. Suddenly the house had "potential" written all over it. Back in the kitchen my coffee had turned cold, but I brewed a fresh pot.

16. Wild West City

The specter of neglected home maintenance continued to haunt me into the summer. As I lounged in my hammock or used it as a net to capture my children, the noise of hammering and sawing by industrious neighbors came to my ears the way the sounds of gallows-construction filter into the adobe cell of a horse thief sentenced to hang.

The ladder had been leaning against our house for three months awaiting ideal atmospheric conditions. And like a condemned man, I knew that one day I'd have to climb that ladder and pay the price that society demands.

But when July 17 dawned sunny and unseasonably crisp and cool, it was much too nice a day to spend fussing over our ruined house. Besides, it was my birthday so I indulged a longstanding desire—we went to an old amusement park in North Jersey called Wild West City.

Betsy had been there twenty years earlier with her parents. I hadn't been so lucky. My parents' tastes ran more toward genuine historic sites or at best scrupulously re-created oldtime villages where on the right day you might get to see flax spun into yarn.

Wild West City consists of two rows of cowtown-style buildings, about two dozen, all told, facing each other across a wide, sandy street lined with hitching rails. The buildings are either working souvenir or snack shops, or Western-type buildings, such as a marshal's office with barred windows, in which children are welcome to play.

Every fifteen minutes or so the public-address system would warn everyone to get safely behind the hitching rails. Then adults in Western clothes would perform a drama on the streets, usually involving hard-ridden horses and lots of blank ammunition fired from real guns. Marie was, at first, disturbed to see grown men fall down and lie motionless in the sand, playing dead, as these playlets unfolded. Corny narration and even prerecorded dialogue came over the public-address system.

The only vehicles on the premises were a horse-drawn stagecoach (rides $1) and a narrow-gauge train (same price) which traveled a circuit through some woods.

Both the train and the stagecoach were subject to holdups by armed badmen. I don't remember exactly how these robberies were transacted because my senses were clouded by embarrassment. I enjoy live entertainment, but I want to be safely separated from it. I even hate it when a performer at a concert tries to get the audience to clap in rhythm. I feel like I'm being put on the spot. So when the man in the black hat brandishing a six-gun climbed up onto the stagecoach and asked me if I had any gold, I could only grit my teeth and look down at my shoes. Maybe he thought I was "yella," but I feel the same way when someone I know suddenly picks up a guitar and puts heart and soul into a song for my listening pleasure.

Marie was a little afraid of the highwaymen and Sally didn't get it at all. She was intrigued by the horses, though. To her fifteen-month-old brain they seemed to be outsize dogs and once she got over her amazement, she woofed at them whenever one was ridden past or when we found some at a hitching rail.

Just about every child on the place had a cap-gun and their desultory snapping would peak during the staged shootouts in the street as boys and girls in the audience would lend their meager firepower to the melodrama as the most peripheral of supporting actors. No one was spared the attentions of these kids. One boy, clicking a toy rifle at little Sally, was told sharply by Betsy, "Don't shoot my baby!"

It was as if the self-conscious enlightenment following the Vietnam era had never intervened between the gun-happy '50s of my youth and the current bloodthirsty age. But because the guns were largely the six-guns and carbines I'd played with thirty years ago instead of the military hardware our neighbor Billy was usually packing, for me the effect was nostalgic.

Except for the big dogs, Sally was immune to the romance of the Old West. Her main interest was in breaking free of parental restraint every chance she got in order to sit down in the deep sand of the street and massage it into her scalp. Or she'd find a puddle near a watering trough or under a faucet and drop to her knees beside it to drink like a dying prospector at a waterhole.

Four-year-old Marie appreciated the cowboy motif, though she had trouble understanding which elements of Wild West City were real. Real horses, fake cowboys, real guns, fake gunfights, etc. And if this isn't the real Wild West, does such a place exist? (A week earlier she'd asked me over lunch, "Is this real or is it a dream?" so I didn't expect her to figure out Wild West City in just one afternoon.)

We bought her a red-felt cowboy hat and she looked so wonderful I took several photos of her—climbing on a big rock, wringing her hands in front of a couple of dead gunslingers, and sitting on a real pony.

The pony ride had been hard to achieve—first we had to wait for tickets because the ticket girl in the little train depot was doubling as the ice-cream scooper in an adjacent shop and she had a busload of Brownie Scouts to satisfy. Finally, ticket in hand, we had to wait because the pony-ride girl had to change clothes and perform in the cancan dance, the only one of the shows in town not involving firearms. (Performed by three fifteen-year-old girls in fishnet stockings, the cancan dance was not put across with the necessary lascivious abandon and I complained about it to my unsympathetic wife. After all, I *was* the Birthday Boy.)

After a few hours we'd skimmed off the cream of the Wild West City experience and Betsy announced it was time to leave. The little pardners didn't object. To Sally, dirt was dirt and the stuff in her own backyard compared favorably with any. Marie was too tired to resist.

But I hated to go. Amid the low-tech fun generated by cheap labor, painted wood, gunpowder, and horse-flesh, I felt like I'd stumbled onto a final remnant of the fifties of my childhood. A place where "bang-you're-dead!" is a phrase free of antisocial connotations; where bad guys wear black hats and are gunned down without being read their rights; and where Roy Rogers is King of the Cowboys instead of a chain of fast-food joints.

Like the 1880s and like the 1950s, Wild West City can't last forever. The high price of land and the demand for housing, coupled with the competition of slick multimillion dollar amusement parks, are closing in. I read in the newspaper that a gang of land developers and condo builders is headed for Wild West City aiming to tear up the town. I've got half a mind to strap on my old six-shooter with the rosewood grips and go do what a man's gotta do. But I've got a wife and children to think about.

17. Hitting Back

Marie, at age four, understood that it is wrong to hit anyone. The few times she was faced with physical aggression, she'd come running to a grownup to register a tearful complaint. And this worked pretty well until the summer she ran afoul of a three-year-old blonde named Pammy.

Marie had befriended Pammy's four-year-old sister Courtney, which left Pammy on the outside-looking-in when the big girls were playing together. So whenever her dark muse stirred, Pammy would come up to Marie and give her a push or a smack. Marie, true to her training, would burst into tears and come running to her nearest parent to weep, whine, and complain.

Maybe it's my darn testosterone, but I found this to be almost as unattractive as Pammy's violence. Along about that time I found an article in a parenting magazine entitled "When Is It OK for Johnny to Hit Back?" It was written by a man with professional credentials. I read it all the way through only to find out that it's never okay for Johnny to hit back. There were a few pacifist strategies for Johnny to try, but if the author had his way, Johnny would be buzzard bait before he'd be permitted to put up his dukes. It should be noted that the National Safety Council says: Don't hit back. Of course they would say that. But if there existed a Preschool Dignity Council, a dissenting opinion might be forthcoming.

Personally, I subscribe to the Judeo-Christian ethic—turn the other cheek to your abuser a couple of times, and if that fails, knock him down and step on him.

So one night, when the kids were asleep and Betsy and I were pillow-talking, I petitioned for a change in policy. "I'd like to tell Marie that it's okay to hit back sometimes. The way she comes crying and tattling to us every time Pammy hits her is disgusting. I'd like to make her a little more self-sufficient."

Betsy agreed reluctantly and with the proviso that when I lay out the new policy for Marie, I limit retaliatory strikes to children old enough to know better (ages three and up) and that I do not mention Pammy by name. In case of a followup investigation by Pammy's mother, she did not want Marie to say, "Daddy told me to hit Pammy."

Before I got a chance to set forth the new rules to Marie, I happened to ask a co-worker, Joni, if she'd ever been in a physical fight when she was a youngster. A strange smile lit her face and she indicated that this was not an anecdote to be blurted out at the water cooler, but a tale to unfold at leisure over lunch. Later, in the cafeteria, she told me this story:

One day when Joni was an eighth grader, she walked out of school to go home when she was accosted by Donna, a girl she barely knew, who accused her of stealing her boyfriend. Not only had Joni not stolen the boyfriend, she wouldn't have taken him as a gift and she said so, as a crowd of thrill-seekers gathered around the two girls. Donna was not satisfied by this and demanded that Joni fight her. (I'd seen this kind of situation often in women-in-prison movies, so I could picture it easily.) But wanting no part of Donna and her love-life and fearing reprisals from school authorities, Joni refused to fight, turned her back on

Donna and the onlookers, and headed for home. But Donna followed her, taunting, shoving, and plucking at her shirt until Joni dropped her textbooks and administered a tentative left to the midsection followed by a large, roundhouse right to the face which ended the fight before it even got going. By the time Joni had picked up her books, Donna was tearfully hotfooting it for home.

And when Donna got there, her father, who happened to be a karate instructor, saw her tear-streaked face and the beginnings of a black eye and asked what had happened. When she told him, the enraged martial artist loaded her into his car and went looking for Joni, who was still walking home. Donna's dad found her and sicced his daughter on her, shouting things like "Trip her! Use your knee! Get her in a headlock!" as the two girls tangled and then rolled on the sidewalk.

(At this point in the story, my eyes were wide open in horrified amazement, but Joni smiled nostalgically.) Apparently Donna was a poor student because Joni listened to the advice meant for her attacker and applied it to demolish Donna again in Round 2. It is to the father's credit that he didn't take on Joni himself, but maybe he was afraid of her. Joni just stood up, adjusted her clothing, picked up her much abused books and continued on her way.

Now, *that's* a story! At first I could hardly believe that a grown man could behave that way. Then, thinking some more about the father, I began to wonder exactly what his daughter told him when she got home. If she had made her father believe that Joni had started it, his reaction wasn't so outlandish after all. This was a cautionary tale for me.

At home after work Betsy told me that Pammy had again sent Marie, the human punching-bag, whimpering for redress to the adults. So when I put Marie to bed, I informed her of the new rules. "For real?" she asked.

"Yes," I said, "Sometimes you have to teach a kid that it is not okay to hit you. But remember, you can hit someone only when they hit you first and only if the child is old enough to know better."

"Is Pammy old enough?" Marie asked, getting right down to cases.

"Yes."

Fifteen hours later Marie, Courtney, and Pammy were in our backyard seated around the picnic table eating lunch. The moms and I were chatting in the kitchen. At the sound of aggrieved weeping, we ran outside. Pammy was sitting on the ground under the picnic table. Marie and Courtney were quietly munching their peanut butter and jelly sandwiches. "What happened?" Pammy's mother asked as she fished her child out from under the table.

As casual as Wyatt Earp blowing the smoke from the barrel of his Buntline Special, Marie looked up from her lunch and said, "Oh, Pammy pushed me, so I pushed her back." The warrant for the violence had been issued by Daddy himself and Marie had no other qualm.

(There's a postscript to this chapter that I'm tempted to leave out because it sounds too pat. Two weeks later at the swim club, Marie was sitting on a big inflated turtle which Pammy was pulling happily through the septic waters of the wading pool. "What's this?" I asked Betsy and she told me that ever since the picnic-table incident Pammy had become Marie's friend. Just like Robin Hood and Little John. And in the year since then, the three girls have played together beautifully. But if you can't believe it, just let it go.)

So, when is it okay for Johnny to hit back? When the other kid is asking for it and fate has selected Johnny to supply it. I should note, though, that Marie and Joni were both lucky. Every time I was nominated to teach somebody a lesson, the other kid was always too big and powerful to learn much.

18. Love feat

May 11, 1969. I was seventeen years old and in love, or something very much like it. The sun was shining and I was walking my girlfriend home from school, blissfully holding her hand.

Suddenly from out of nowhere a little girl on a bike showed up beside us. "Why don't you kiss her?" she taunted and kept on taunting in the same vein, riding her bike in slow, looping circles in the quiet street, so as to match our progress.

This embarrassed me a great deal, though my girlfriend didn't seem to care. I didn't want to open a discussion with the child, so I just tried to ignore her, hoping she'd go away. But she soon explained, "I don't have anything to do, so I'm going to follow you wherever you go."

I was reminded of this scene one sultry midnight in August. Betsy and I were in bed about to conduct a transaction of love when, from the corner of my eye, I discerned a small person standing in the doorway. The noise from the ceiling fan had covered the sounds of Marie's approach.

"We've got company," I told Betsy as Marie piped up, "Can I come into bed, too?"

"I don't think so," I said, pretty sure there were state laws to back me up. Betsy got up, robed herself, and escorted Marie back to her own room.

I was relieved to find out later that Marie had no inkling of what we were doing. In fact, it happens so infrequently that *I* hardly knew what we were doing.

The sad truth is, that the mom-dad love feat requires special circumstances: Both children must be completely asleep and both parents must be partially awake. It's like a NASA space mission—ever-shifting atmospheric and celestial conditions must line up just right to afford that fleetingly open "window of opportunity."

In our marriage, that "window" is all the more fleeting because of my work schedule. Half the time I was getting home from work at two a.m., an hour at which Betsy is, understandably, as frisky as Trigger the stuffed horse and does not want to wake up.

And on the rare occasions when we are both awake in bed, there is a more pressing need that must be satisfied—the need to hold an adult conversation without being interrupted.

This is often the time for intense parenting strategy sessions, trying to come up with ways to mold the behavior of our children into happier channels. Like Dr. Frankenstein and Igor in a desperate huddle, speaking low so as not to awaken the experiments-gone-awry.

Other times our love trysts resemble club meetings. Old business first: "So, what did the doctor say about the baby's cough?" Then new business: "Rick, I've applied to Rutgers' library school."

After discussing surprise career plans, the children's health problems, temper tantrums, appliance repairs, upcoming birthday parties, and other manifestations of a world gone mad, it's time for the membership to strip for the social portion of the meeting. That's when it's vital to lock the door—so nonmembers don't witness the secret handshake.

And speaking of unwanted witnesses, how about the child who was pestering me back in '69? A child who, I now realize, was a fragile human being, probably damaged in some unknowable way, trying clumsily, with a child's limited means, to shore up her eroded sense of personhood. What could I do to reach her through her obvious pain and anger?

I don't know what *you* would have done, but I had my own personhood to look after—I picked up stones from the street and threw them at her until she rode away shrieking.

I can't defend my actions of long ago, but I'll admit it's kind of refreshing to remember a moment when my love-life was held hostage and I refused to negotiate.

19. Talking tots

"I hate everybody! I want everybody to hate me! I wish I was killed!" These antisocial remarks were delivered at full volume by Marie in November about a month before her fifth birthday.

I don't remember the exact context of her statement except that she and her mother were having some kind of disagreement and it was not a happy moment to be in our lovely home. But I do remember my mixed feelings of the moment—anxiety about Marie's negative streak and admiration of her ability to express herself fully and precisely.

It's no accident that this book begins with an eighteen-month gap. Lamentable, but it's all for the best; I haven't got anything to say about babies. I'll admit to marveling at the miracle of Baby Marie's tiny fingers and toes and admiring the spherical perfection of her moon head, but beyond that I'd have to say that babies are all maintenance and potential, putting forward very little in the way of performance.

At one point during Marie's infancy, Betsy said to me, "Do you realize that you never talk to her? She'll never learn to talk if people don't talk to her." I was abashed and thenceforth forced myself to talk to Baby Marie. Naturally, most of what I said was goofy and immaterial and I had a fear Marie would learn to talk *that* way and chatter her way through life like a Little League infielder. Nobatter, nobatter, humbabe, humbabe.

When Baby Sally came along, I was a fair hand at baby-chatter—good enough to give my big brother Steve a lesson in it, anyway. Steve is an academic type, an archaeologist, and doesn't have much to do with babies, dogs, and other noncerebrals unless they were part of a pre-Columbian culture.

At a big family dinner we were all sitting around the table at my dad's house. Steve's wife Eleanor was pregnant with their first child, so Steve was trying awkwardly to get some hands-on experience with six-month-old Sally. He was holding her in the same formal, careful way you would hold somebody else's melting ice-cream cone.

I'm enough of a little brother to take delight in advising Steve on the two or three subjects about which I know more. "Go ahead and talk to her," I suggested, knowing it would never cross his mind to do so.

He peered down at the drooling, grinning creature he was holding at arm's length and replied, "What?"

"Steve," I said patiently, presenting Betsy's wisdom as my own, "babies need to be spoken to. When your baby's born, you're going to have to talk to her a lot or she'll never learn the language."

"You're right, of course," he said, and examined Sally's chubby face for some clue as to a topic of mutual interest. But nothing was forthcoming.

"It's easy," I told him. "It doesn't matter what you say, just so long as you say it in a friendly way. Start in anywhere. See what she's wearing? React to it. Tell her what color it is. How about her hair? Describe it. 'My, don't you have a fuzzy head of hair!' Don't let yourself feel silly about it; it'll sound right to her, and other adults won't be expecting you to deliver a dissertation on prehistoric metallurgy to a baby."

Steve was too self-conscious to talk to Sally just then, but later in the evening he was off in a corner with her, gamely discussing the size of her hands ("tiny") and her prospects for getting teeth ("any day now").

Pompous speeches to my big brother notwithstanding, Betsy notes that when Marie started learning to talk, my interest in her multiplied. And it happened all over again with Sally. In November at eighteen months of age she had a twenty-word vocabulary that was growing daily.

That's not to say that I didn't love her as a gurgling baby. During the first year of her life she and I developed an affectionate rapport that was generally nonverbal. There was lots of smiling and tickling and petting and patting. And of course lots of that one-way small-talk from me.

When she began saying real words, it was as if a pet I'd known and loved for years began developing the power of speech.

Sally's newfound speaking ability was all the more novel because it was so incongruous with her behavior. She liked to eat off the floor, rip apart books, and leap from high places. Sally's idea of table manners was to climb up onto the table and throw crockery onto the floor. She had given up eating dirt, but still liked to drink from puddles. (Health note: It may seem like a natural and ecologically sound idea, but this can be bad for small children. After lapping at the horsed-over sands of Wild West City, Sally suffered a intestinal disorder that lasted for weeks and gave the nursery the air of a biological weapons test range.)

While engaged in her acts of household vandalism, she'd be saying either "uh-oh" or "no." She had mastered the meaning of "uh-oh" well enough and she said it with a properly doleful expression, though it hadn't dawned on her yet that these regrettable incidents were in any way preventable.

She didn't understand "no" at all. Because she heard it whenever one of those regrettable incidents was occurring, to her it was simply the verbal accompaniment to the action, appropriate whether she'd say it or her parents said it. Sally would be busily hauling at a fully freighted tablecloth and as our plates, glasses, and dinner inched toward the precipice, she and the rest of us would shout a spirited "No!," the way a bullfighter and his fans will all holler "Olé!"

Sally said her first word when she was eleven months old. Heartwarmingly enough, she was calling her big sister, rendering "Marie" as "Weewee!" Marie was charmed by this pronunciation at first but after a few months the novelty wore off and she was relieved when Sally's diction improved and her name was spoken pretty much the way a competent adult would say it.

Marie never realized how close she'd come to joining the legions of older siblings who have been grotesquely renamed by babies. My sister-in-law Laura went through high school as "Wawa" because of my wife's early ham-tongued attempts at speech. I know a forty-year-old man who is still known in the greater Trenton area as "Tojie" because his baby brother couldn't say "Tony." And I recently learned of a grown man named Gary who is still called "Beez-doo" in some circles.

Just as I enjoy a talking child, my wife prefers a preverbal child. Like anyone, four-year-old Marie was saying a lot that was inane or boring—dumb questions like "How can you tell when it's night?" and banal remarks like "What do you think of all this rain?" and long, detailed descriptions of what her friends did and said.

But mixed in with the low-grade ore were good questions like: "Why don't shadows have shadows?" and "Is money important?" and "What's the most important word in the world?"

And funny rejoinders—for example, upon being told that her late great-grandfather spoke with a Scottish accent like Scrooge McDuck's, Marie asked, "But Daddy, how can you talk when you're dead?"

Or dialogue like this:

Marie (an hour after defeat in a game of Candy-
land): Daddy, when I lost the game, I got very
sad.
Me: I know, sweetie. Most kids feel that way.
Marie: In fact, all of them?

Or this:

Marie (walking with me through a field of tall
corn): Daddy, isn't this where we saw the
snake?
Me: No, he was four or five rows over.
Marie: Five, I hope.

Even taking the dull with the sharp, Marie's chit-
chat continues to be music to me and I could listen
to her all day. At least I feel like I could. But I don't
have to; I'm at work all day. Betsy is home all day.
Sometimes when I come home and Marie is nattering
along in her bright, engaging way, or Sally is reliving
for the two hundredth time an incident in which she
was sprayed with soapy water through a half-open
window at the carwash, Betsy will catch my eye and
make a pistol out of her right hand, put it to her temple
and pantomime suicide.

Betsy is too much of a good sport to suggest that
we get rid of our kids as they learn to talk. But she
has suggested that we produce another one and I sus-
pect that she's motivated by the prospect of enjoying
at least a year of nonprattling companionship. Maybe
what she really needs is a dog.

20. Parties

A dozen five-year-olds were upstairs in our house running from room to room, screaming and bumping into things. Betsy's vigilance had slipped momentarily and Marie's birthday party had spun out of control. As helpful as a fly-on-the-wall, I followed Betsy as she ran briskly up the stairs. One of the smaller kids lay on the threshold of our bedroom, overwrought, crying, possibly injured, and in danger of being trampled by three-way traffic swirling past and over him.

This would have been the time to point a gun at the ceiling and fire a shot, but Betsy is above crude barroom theatrics. In a loud, but friendly voice she commanded, "Okay! Everybody lie down on the floor!" Sensing fun in the air, every kid lay down.

"What now?" I asked Betsy as twelve little bodies quivered expectantly on the carpet.

"A peanut hunt," she said. The order to lie down had been only a ploy to stop their running and get their attention. Like airplanes, children need momentum to remain in flight.

The peanut hunt was a big hit and so was "tape the tail on the donkey." (What kind of reckless, barbaric parents did we have, who would blindfold a child, arm him with a straight pin and send him forth to impale whatever he encountered?)

Another diversion, which Betsy had found in a book, was the making of "peanut catchers." You stick an unsharpened pencil through a paper cup and you tie one end of a string to the pencil and one end to a peanut. Then the fun-seeker holds the cup and tries to flip the peanut into the cup. I like to think I know something about fun, but I'd made one of these the night before and tried it out. Where the fun entered into this pointless activity, I couldn't see and I told Betsy so. But she ignored my input and sure enough, the peanut-catchers were an absorbing and intriguing part of the two-hour round of delights for which Betsy was the producer, director, and ringmaster.

Not everyone has my wife's good sense and skill at throwing a party. A couple of months previously a co-worker friend named Janet had asked me if I had any Halloween videotapes that she could show at her four-year-old son's party. Somewhat self-righteously I urged, "Come on, you can keep those kids busy for a couple of hours without videotapes. Make 'em do things." Once again I was spouting Betsy's teachings as my own.

She took my advice and reported good results. (But it should be noted that two months later, Janet threw a Christmas party for grownups which centered around a showing of *It's a Wonderful Life* on the living-room TV set and a program of professional wrestling on a portable in the kitchen. Although the hostess had done an admirable job of finding something for everyone on only two TV sets, we had to leave early because I didn't want everyone to see me cry when all the townspeople bring money to Jimmy Stewart.)

Getting back to birthday parties, the biggest ones are thrown when the firstborn reaches age one and a houseful of adults is invited. This party is an important rite of passage for new parents. It is the event at which they realize that they no longer have much in common with their childless friends and that even their parent friends are more excited by the hors d'oeuvres than by Junior's big milestone.

Thanks to this insight and because Junior doesn't

yet have any friends of his own, his next birthday and will be celebrated with more restraint—like a reception that follows a bride's third wedding.

But when the kids' parties resume in earnest at age three or so, they can be hard to keep under control and in perspective. For school-age kids, the more sophisticated pleasures afforded by birthday-party package deals at movie theaters, zoos, museums, or roller rinks might be in order. But my wife takes preschool birthday parties as a special challenge to her imagination and her good sense.

Her guiding principle may invite challenge and debate, but it has served her well and is worth considering: "What little kids would really like to do is eat cake and ice cream and then go outside and throw dirt at each other. So keep it simple."

21. Feeding Time

Like my parents, I place great emphasis on the family dinner—a happy and peaceful interlude, where children and parents discuss the events of the day, affection and merriment abound, and good food is eaten politely and appreciatively.

Of course I've never had one of those family dinners, not then and not now, but the possibility draws me forward from supper to supper, like a mirage luring a thirsty Foreign Legionnaire from dune to dune.

Let me provide some deep background on family dining. (I very nearly passed a college course in anthropology, so I am somewhat credentialed in this area.) The first human beings used to spend their days wandering around, finding and eating berries, roots, and bugs, returning to their dens at night to sleep. The only time a family ate together was when something had died that was too large for one person to eat. Then they'd swarm around the carcass, grunting and snapping their teeth, jabbing each other with sticks, grabbing for the choicest cuts or meatiest bones.

Take away the appetites and you've got dinner at our house, as practiced by Sally the winter she was almost two. You see, kids still have the genetic memories they were born with. They feed all day on whatever they can get their paws on, so when Mom and Dad try to get them to come to dinner and force them to eat more than they have use for, all they want to do is escape—leap down onto the floor and scurry away to their dens.

Betsy and I had tried starving Sally a little bit before dinner to attune her to our agenda. But this only caused her to come early to the dinner table, crawl under it, and graze upon the crumbs and crusts she found under there.

Besides her general rioting and fraternity food-fight manners, Sally had two main dinnertime themes in that unhappy season. She wanted only what was on someone else's plate. And even that food would lose its desirability the instant it would arrive by fork in the air-space over her own plate.

Her other theme was the expression of a burning desire to sit on a parental lap while we ate. We never let her do it. Nevertheless she'd stand up on her booster seat for half the meal and repeatedly yell "Mommy!" or "Daddy!" depending on which one she thought would want to wrestle a wild monkey while trying to ply knife and fork.

Marie, just turned five, was much further along

the evolutionary path. She was still capable of kicking her sister under the table and would sometimes goad her to a shrieking frenzy, but Marie's main contribution to the evening stressfest in those days was less violent. You see, Marie doesn't like vegetables, meat, or potatoes. What else is there? Not much except dessert.

My wife had spent half her own childhood sitting alone at the table after dinner contemplating a nauseating little pile of lima beans, so our house rule has always been: "No child will be forced to eat." But its corollary is: "No dessert unless you do a good job on your dinner."

This rule provided Marie with her theme as she turned suppertime into one protracted negotiating session as we'd hammer out exactly what constitutes "a good job" on dinner. She'd take a couple tentative bites of her spaghetti and then demand, "What's the ticket to dessert?"

From the other side of the bargaining table her mother would say, "Three forkfuls of spaghetti, two pieces of broccoli, and the rest of your milk."

To put this opening bid into context, Marie would then want to know what we'd be having for dessert. If it was only an apple, Marie would try to renegotiate the intake requirements or simply put down her tools and strike. But for a cookie, she'd dig in gamely and purposefully.

Luckily I wasn't burdened with the authority to set the terms of the contract, but sometimes I'd be given the delicate job of determining exactly how many linear inches of spaghetti add up to a forkful. (Sally's food was never measured by the forkful in those days because to put a fork anywhere near her would be to invite tragedy.)

Those mealtimes with their mingled ambiance of

feeding time at the zoo and hard-bargaining with the Teamsters eventually mellowed, but I have yet to realize my dream of sitting down to suppers at which the chef is complimented, the meal is consumed with gusto, and feelings of warmth and togetherness turn our dining room into a true temple of love.

The fact is, this kind of harmony is within easy reach. But Betsy says breast-feeding is out of the question.

22. The perfect father

My father was perfect. In his whole life he never stole, never drank to excess, never smoked, never cursed, never quarreled with my mother, never made a bigoted remark, never cheated on his income taxes, and never returned a library book late.

As a lad in the 1920s he never threw horse manure at his playmates and as an adult he never faked a sick call to work. He would no sooner steal a hotel towel than he would commit a triple ax-murder.

Though I admired his adherence to the straight and narrow path, I was never a hundred percent comfortable with this kind of father. I felt that his moderate lifestyle and apparent freedom from temptation prevented him from fully appreciating the kind of lively and adventuresome boy that I was for the first thirty years of my life. My antics, which ranged from playing with firecrackers in early days to stealing rides on freight trains later on, included nothing really evil. My specialty was foolish, dangerous, victimless stuff.

With a couple of kids of my own, I'm groping to

find the right level of virtue to project as Betsy and I try to shape them into people who will be happy, healthy, safe, and sane.

"Daddy, I can't sleep." It was a cold, winter night—ideal for sleeping, especially in our old house where bed is the only warm place. Nevertheless, for the fifth night in a row, Marie had been read to, snuggled with, and tucked in, but had rematerialized in the living room.

Now, according to our routine, I would guide her back upstairs, put her back into her bed and urge her to lie still with eyes closed and think about how much her mommy and daddy love her. This is the mental equivalent of warm milk; no child can hold this thought for five full seconds and remain awake.

But this time, feelings of camaraderie got the better of me and I confided to her, "Y'know, Marie, when I was a little kid I used to do exactly what you're doing at bedtime. And my mom would give me a kiss and send me back to bed. That's what I went downstairs for—just a little extra love from my mom." My eyes grew misty at this recollection of my sweet, departed mother.

That bit of sentiment cost us an evening of peace. On the strength of my chummy little speech, Marie felt emboldened to make four more curtain calls that evening, and the only thing that finally kept her in her bed was a snarled threat of personal injury from my lovely wife.

Maybe one spate of small-caliber misbehavior is not much to draw from, but a general principle of parent-child dynamics seemed to be at work and it wasn't hard to figure out: When a child does something undesirable, it doesn't help for a parent to say, "Gee, I used to do that, too. Care to hear about it?"

Luckily Marie was not yet old enough to appreciate stories of her daddy's truancy, deceptions, and disobedience, or I might have blabbed them to her in a well-meaning effort to cement our friendship and bolster her self-esteem.

Recanting that testimony later could be awkward:

"Marie, what makes you think that I used to tease my little brother when I was your age? *I* told you that? Oh no, you must have misunderstood. I used to *please* my little brother. You see, Marie, I knew how much my parents prized a peaceful and harmonious household, so I would shower my little brother with gifts and other kindnesses. Come to think of it, you might want to try that with your little sister."

Or: "Uh, Marie, remember when I told you that when I was in the third grade I used to pretend to be sick so I could stay home from school? Well, I was only joking. It was someone else who did that. A wicked little boy . . . named . . . uh . . . Tommy. Yes, Tommy. A terrible thing about poor Tommy. Yes, his dad discovered he had been only faking and forced him to go to school anyhow. But it turns out that time he really was sick. No matter how much he moaned and complained, no one would believe him. Finally, just after recess, his mysterious ailment brought his blood to a full boil and poor Tommy died. With my own record of perfect attendance, of course I was there to hear his final words. Tommy said, 'This is what I deserve for fibbing to my dear parents.' "

What I realized then is the need to find a way to let Marie know that she's not going through life alone. But at the same time, I want her to look upon her father as something a little more uplifting than a mere co-conspirator.

I guess the ideal father would have kind of a

priestly persona; he'd come across as someone who personally doesn't sin, but is equipped nevertheless to understand and counsel those who do.

A kindly providence had given me a first child who is well behaved, cautious, and courteous. I knew I'd better make my mistakes on Marie because I could tell early on that Sally would not be giving me much leeway. A couple of months shy of her second birthday, Sally's idea of a good time was to throw onto the floor everything she could reach. Then she'd get a chair and happily harvest the next-higher stratum of stuff, singing or cheering all the while. At mealtimes a spoon and a dish were her javelin and discus. In her more studious moments she'd sit down with a book and joyously play a ripping-good game of "she loves me, she loves me not" with its pages.

After taking stock of my lively and adventuresome secondborn, I decided upon immediate rebirth as the paragon of virtue that my dad was. And I'm a better man for it.

23. Punishment

In olden times, each royal child would be given a non-royal child for a playmate. Once their friendship was established, the pal would receive any spankings earned by the royal child. When Princess Marie was born, I assumed that we would acquire a whipping boy so we could administer disciplinary thrashings without defiling the royal flesh.

But Betsy, who sets policy on everything that matters, told me that wouldn't be necessary because there would be no disciplinary thrashings—ours would be a No-Spanking Household. Because parents should set an example of nonviolence, Little Marie would have her behavior modified and her character developed through more subtle means, poor kid.

I remember that as a child I'd always preferred a good, brisk spanking to a long drawnout lecture on how I'd once again disappointed my incurably optimistic parents. Of course I never got to choose my punishment, but now that I look back, I have a feeling that I could have, if I'd come forward with some solid recommendations.

My wife and her four siblings grew up secure in the knowledge that they'd have their behinds smacked with Mom's wooden spoon if they misbehaved. But my brothers and I never knew what to expect. It seems there was a different punishment each time. It was my lot to experience the traditional over-the-knee spanking; the quick, angry slap at the dinner table; banishment to my room; suspension of TV privileges; the aforementioned heart-to-heart talk; and, of course, house arrest.

Looking back, my brother Jim has the impression that our parents were experimenting to find the perfect punishment—one so effective that it would only have to be meted out once and we'd never be bad again. Aside from capital punishment, I don't think such a disciplinary treatment exists. In any case, our folks never discovered it.

Once at age five, I socked another kid on the jaw and I had to sit in the kitchen for ten full minutes. One time at dinner, to ensure the pleasure of my company for the entire meal, I was tied into my chair with a dishtowel. (This was more of a practical restraint than a true punishment, plus it was kind of fun.) Even more than my mom, my mild-mannered dad was really out of his depth when it came to punishing us. Once, when I was ten or twelve, he sentenced me to write an essay on the meaning of the word "moderation." (I can't remember of what excess I'd been guilty.)

Also around that time, after months of threatening to spank me *with a belt*, some low deed of mine served to call my dad's bluff and I was hauled upstairs and made to lie down on the bed. Even though my pants had been left up, I didn't like the idea of being beaten with a weapon; it seemed like a dangerous precedent. I could tell that my dad wasn't comfortable with it either. He'd apparently been hoping he'd never have to sink to this level of brutality, and the feebleness of his blows proved it. For all the terror and pain they induced, I could have cracked open a schoolbook and done some homework right there under the lash.

But I had the good sense to scream and writhe as if my dad were a black-hooded inquisitor wielding a cat-o'-nine-tails. I was never whipped again. The belt threat was replaced by a new one—if I didn't shape up, I'd be sent away to a military academy. I knew that cadets wore uniforms and marched in formation and I suspected that they got to sleep in tents and shoot rifles. But I was smart enough to keep these thoughts to myself.

Anyhow, the result of this smorgasbord of punishment was a well-developed sense of right and wrong, but no special inclination in either direction.

So when Betsy set forth a strong disciplinary policy, I was eager to get behind it. The no-hitting stricture is just a minor element of a carefully balanced code of coercion, compulsion, manipulation, and motivation. The main principles are: 1. Don't make idle threats; 2. Rewards work better than punishments;

3. A parental "no" must never be successfully whined into a "maybe."

After I'd mentioned our no-spank policy to a co-worker, she happened to introduce me to her adolescent son. She told him, "You'd like to live in *his* house; he doesn't believe in discipline." I fought down an urge to turn her over my knee then and there.

Not only do we have discipline, we even have punishment. But at its best, it is low-key and undramatic. First Marie gets warned. Then she gets reprimanded. Then she gets sent to her room where she is ignored until one of her parents feels like going up and grinding her into submission and repentance with a long, boring sermon much like the ones I used to dread so much. Like a saddle horse with a sensitive mouth, Marie, at age five, needs only the lightest pressure on the figurative reins to guide her back onto the paths of righteousness.

Sally, on the other hand, can take a good, strong tongue-lashing and continue off course. When that happens, we have no choice but to cage her. Secured in her crib she'll rage for ten or twenty minutes, after which she is usually ready to be held, patted, kissed, and paroled. I have no idea how our policy of nonviolence will hold up as Sally grows too big for her cage.

24. Secondborn

So what's wrong with Sally? Why is she such a handful?

When Marie was born, she instantly became the center of her mother's universe and, more gradually, mine too. Three years later, when Sally came along, she found the job market had tightened up. There's nothing wrong with Sally; she's just a secondborn child and that's not a job you can do sitting down.

She sings. She dances. She puts a colander on her head and wears it like a helmet. She shouts, "Done!" and hurls a plate of food onto the floor. She scribbles on the wall. She throws chalk into the toilet. She claims her name is Jessica (a cousin) and tells you there's a monster on your head.

If you dumped out a puzzle in front of Marie when she was a tot, maybe she'd cry in frustration, but she'd try to assemble it. Sally would just look at the pieces; they would awaken no internal spirit of cooperation causing her to want to put them together for you.

Recent studies indicate that birth order has a lot more to do with a child's personality than had been supposed. The experts could've saved themselves some research if they had thought to ask me.

Years ago, working for the *Delaware Valley News,* I went to photograph Lenore O'Reilly, a teenager who had won some distinction in a beauty pageant. At the O'Reilly home, the mom was fussing over Lenore, getting her ready for the picture, while the tomboy-looking kid sister sulked conspicuously nearby. "I guess I'll never get my picture in the paper," she said hopelessly.

"Now Bonnie," her mom said, soothingly while brushing the big sister's bangs into formation. "Both you girls do different things. Lenore does well in these pageants, but you have special talents." She groped briefly and offered, "Like the way you play the flute so nicely."

"*Mom!*" Bonnie yelled in anguish, making two syllables out of the word. "*Lenore* plays the flute; I play the clarinet." She ran down the hall and demonstrated a flair for percussion, too, with a good, resonant slam of her bedroom door.

A second child myself, I gave Mrs. O'Reilly an accusatory look. I considered following Bonnie to her room and sharing with her the idea that firstborns are mere "practice children" who are frequently ruined by overdoses of parental love and attention which render them nervous, selfish, conceited, and arrogant. But instead I held my tongue and photographed the beauty queen, ironically contributing to the photography imbalance that exists in every home with more than one child.

Every smile, every bath, every cute icicle of saliva hanging from the royal firstborn chin, is captured on film. A second child will get some exposure, but usually sharing the frozen moment with the firstborn. The only time No. 2 seems worth photographing alone is when she manages to get into Mommy's makeup or do something really special to herself with mud or chocolate cake. Although these pictures will embarrass her later, at the time they reinforce the idea that attention is earned by acting up.

A third or fourth child generally won't be photographed at all until he's eligible for a school photo or a shutterbug uncle rounds up all the kids at a family reunion for a group photo.

The frequent photography of the firstborn is part of the intense interest that helps turn them into great achievers. But they achieve because they are pushed—like unhappy surfers propelled forward atop a surging wave of parental expectation and anxiety. When secondborns achieve, it's because they are drawn toward enterprise and exertion as the means of obtaining a tiny share of the emotional and material goodies that the firstborn gets automatically. Secondborns must hustle for what they get.

Secondborns are further challenged by a few other factors.

We are starved for recognition. Child No. 1 takes his first step and Mom and Dad want to call a press conference. Child No. 2 takes his first step and there are yawns all around and although no one says it, deep down Mom and Dad feel that he's plagiarizing Child No. 1. In terms of parental acclaim, the second-born is like the second man to fly solo across the Atlantic, whoever that was. The milestone achievements of the second child are as remarkable as jokes that you've already heard.

Also, we secondborns usually aren't as smart as the firstborns. That's because our parents didn't have the time or the inclination to be stimulating our little brains every waking moment—tickling us, petting us, photographing us, and reading to us. So, to offset our inability to think great thoughts and do calculus, we secondborns must develop other tools, such as personal charm and low animal cunning.

Furthermore, because our parents' obsessive fear has lessened with experience, secondborns do not acquire the exaggerated sense of caution that firstborns have. Consequently, driven to perform daring feats to get attention, secondborns are characteristically prone to injury and disfigurement. My wife (also a secondborn) is a victim of this syndrome and the sad fact is proved anew every time she smiles. She lost part of a front tooth twenty-five years ago in a bike crash—an accident which a more prudent child would have avoided.

And there's a related phenomenon: Parents are

slower to seek medical attention for secondborns. I recall a bicycling mishap of my own in which my forehead came into sharp contact with the curb. I saw stars. My mom didn't rush me to the hospital for x-rays, as she probably would've if it'd been her firstborn who was knocked senseless. But to her credit, she wasn't ready to laugh it off, either. So as sort of a compromise she took me to Mr. Angelotti, a high school biology teacher. He asked me how many fingers he was holding up, pronounced me fit, and that was the end of it. I like to think that if my head injury had been properly treated, I'd be getting as much mail from the Nobel and Pulitzer prize committees as I currently receive from Publishers' Clearing House.

So what does all this add up to for little Sally? I think she'll be okay. As I had wanted to tell Bonnie O'Reilly: In the final analysis, a first child is like a few pounds of meat tossed to a pair of starving tigers. It'll get plenty of attention, but is that necessarily beneficial? That first course takes the edge off the tigers' frenzy. Whatever gets thrown to them next might not get such an enthusiastic reception, but it'll find them a little calmer. And that's good.

25. Wondering about Death

"Daddy, if you made someone a promise and then that person dies, would you have to keep the promise?" Marie was asking another one of her death questions. She had touched on the topic every so often before, but for some reason, during this prekindergarten summer, Marie would address the general phenomenon about once a week. She wasn't worried about death, just curious. And once she'd received an answer or two, her curiosity would subside for awhile.

Before I could answer this week's question, I had to pin it down. "Do you mean, for example, if you promised me you'd never smoke cigars and then I died, would you have to keep your promise about cigars?"

"No," she said, "I mean, if I promised someone I'd go over to visit them, and then they died, would I still have to go?"

Betsy reports another discussion initiated by Marie: "Does a person know ahead of time that they are about to die?"

Betsy replied, "Sometimes it's a surprise, but lots of times a person is so sick that the doctors can't make him better and he knows that he's going to die soon."

"I guess when everyone knows a person is going to die that person gets lots of presents," Marie surmised.

Betsy, already slightly disturbed by the topic, nipped this line of reasoning in the bud: "Actually, when a person knows he is going to die, he usually *gives away* his favorite things to his favorite people."

Another time, shortly after a discussion of summer weather, Marie was coloring at the kitchen table under a ceiling fan while I was nearby emptying the dishwasher. Apparently speaking to her coloring book, Marie said slowly, "Summer, fall, winter, spring. Summer, fall, winter, spring. And over and over and over and over and over again . . ." whereupon she turned to me with a triumphant smile and concluded, "then you die." Yeah, that about sums it up. In this country, where death is deemed unnatural and improper and the culture is locked into the denial mode, it takes an unindoctrinated child to state the obvious. I nodded in agreement with her and Marie resumed her coloring as if she hadn't just said anything special.

Sometimes Marie approaches her favorite topic from the side. One day while we were paddling our canoe down the Delaware, Marie said, "What if no more babies were born?"

"Well," I said, "eventually, everybody would get old and die and there'd be no more people."

"Then would animals live in the houses?" she asked promptly, maybe sensing a big real estate opportunity.

"Do you mean like the Three Little Pigs and the Three Bears walking on hind legs and living like people? Or do you mean like mice and squirrels creeping into an empty house?"

"Mice and squirrels."

"Probably."

"Oh," she said, able to relax and resume her counterproductive back-to-front paddling now that this important loose end had been tied up.

One of Marie's favorite kinds of questions is the "what if." One day we were driving past a cemetery and she asked, "What if you yelled so loud that you woke up the dead people?"

"First of all," I said slowly, giving myself time to think, "I wouldn't do that. Second . . ."

"It wouldn't work," she finished for me, her smile showing she hadn't been serious this time.

In the next session Marie wanted to know about burial procedures. "Do people get buried in a box?" "Why is it called a coffin?" "Do people wear clothes when they get buried?" "Why don't they just throw a dead person into a hole? Nothing can hurt you when you're dead, right?" This last remark, although it contained some admirable practical wisdom, made me decide to put someone more sentimental in charge of my funeral arrangements.

Another day she was back on a more philosophical plane asking, "Does everything have an ending?"

I was in my pajamas drinking coffee in the kitchen. "What kind of things do you mean?" I asked.

"People. Do all people have endings?" I'd already told her that everybody dies sooner or later, so I figured this was an afterlife question, so I told her, "People with children don't die completely. Part of them keeps living in their children and their children's children."

"Oh," she said quietly. I felt kind of bad; a couple of Marie's playmates are going to Heaven when *they* die. The vicarious, absentee immortality I was laying out for Marie is pretty pale stuff by comparison, but it's all I had to offer. Or so I thought, until Marie got a glimpse of an earthly paradise about ten days later.

I was about to go collect the babysitter so Betsy and I could go out to a movie. Marie asked, "If you and Mommy died, who would take care of Sally and me?"

A fair question. "You'd go live with Aunt Laura and Uncle Roger," I said. The previous summer I'd asked them if that would be okay and they'd nervously said yes.

But to Marie the prospect was more than okay. Laura and Roger have three children who are idolized by Marie. Laura and Roger always treat our kids with special kindness and affection. Roger, the proprietor of the Somerville Pet Shop, is a hard worker and an excellent provider and his family lives well in a lovely home. Furthermore, this genial trafficker in bunnies and gerbils has been known to take his work home with him.

Marie's eyes lit up at the prospect and I wished I'd picked a less attractive contingency plan. But Marie had no wizened, gray Uncle Henry and Aunt Em with a windblown farmstead on a dismal prairie; the cheerful opulence of Laura and Roger would have to do. Marie demanded: "How would they know?"

"What do you mean?" I asked.

"If you and Mommy died, how would Aunt Laura and Uncle Roger know to come and get us?" Marie didn't want to miss a minute of the good life.

After a moment's thought, I had to admit that the police would probably make a few phone calls after our bodies were discovered and eventually word would reach Laura and Roger. This conversation was getting too specific, forcing me to imagine men in blue taking a wallet from my corpse to check for ID, but I try never to flinch from a fair question. "I'll tell you what," I said. "I'll put Aunt Laura's phone number on the wall by the phone and if anything happens, you can call her yourself."

"Okay, Daddy. Thanks," she said, with no more emotion other than the trace of gratitude you'd feel for the woman at the dry cleaner's when she hands you your trousers.

For about two weeks, no further reference was made to this chat and I was hoping that Marie had mentally filed this information away under "reassurances." But then she got wind of a special outing her cousins were taking. "Just think, Daddy," she said wistfully, "if you and Mommy were dead, Sally and I would be at the circus right now."

One thing about Marie: You always know what she's thinking.

26. Little Ricky

Marie and I have a game we sometimes play in which Little Ricky (my 1956 self) shows up to visit Marie in the present. Both Marie and Ricky are aware of their future relationship and the magical nature of their meetings. I hope this game is not psychologically dangerous in some way, because I enjoy it. Of course, what I'd *really* like is to be five years old with Marie, in addition to being her father. Playing the Little Ricky game is the best I can do.

In some installments of the game Little Ricky shows up with some little relic (usually found in my father's attic or garage)—my old teddy bear, The Merry Milkman board game, or some Davy Crockett collector's cards.

"This is a picture of Davy Crockett," Little Ricky tells Marie. "My big brother pretends to be him and I pretend to be his pal Georgie."

Although I'd show her a picture of Fess Parker portraying the King of the Wild Frontier, I don't think she could really see him. Jaded as a moth from Las Vegas, she'd spent too much time watching the vivid colors of the cartoon characters on TV, done too much drawing with fluorescent markers in colors like electric green and hot magenta and wearing too much clothing dyed shocking pink and antifreeze yellow. There's no way she could focus on, let alone take an interest in, someone wearing buckskin and a brown fur cap.

Another time, playing our game in the backseat of the car while Betsy drove, Marie learned that when I was little we didn't have seatbelts. The kids would stand on the backseat with elbows on the back of the frontseat, so we could peer through the windshield and breathe into our parents' ears. She was slightly horrified at such unbelted recklessness.

It was my turn to be alarmed when Marie helpfully informed Little Ricky from her modern-day vantage point, "Your mom is going to die."

"Don't tell me that!" I said with real dismay, though remaining in character.

Of all the news from the past that Little Ricky shared with Marie, the most interesting material was about the pioneer days of televiewing. "Where I'm from, when you turn on the TV, you have to wait about two minutes for it to warm up before you can see anything," I told her.

"How long is two minutes?" Marie asked, and I showed her, maintaining one hundred and twenty seconds of silence.

"Also, we don't have color; only black-and-white." (She had seen reruns of *Lassie* and *Mr. Ed* but apparently had thought that the blue-gray color was some unpleasant, experimental new effect. "How'd they get it gray?" she had asked.)

"And there are only three channels. On Saturday mornings when we get up really early, there's no Disney Channel with cartoons and good stuff for kids," I said, Little Ricky's remarks finding a rapt audience. "We're stuck watching a boring show for farmers."

"Besides that, we don't have a VCR to tape a show when we're going to be away. But my dad wouldn't tape a show anyway because he'd never been a TV-watching kid so he doesn't care about TV. He and my mom are always interrupting shows to call us to dinner or to do something else that could easily wait until a commercial."

The impact of this information broke up our game

and Little Ricky vanished as Marie said, "Daddy, I'm glad I didn't have to live during the old days," sounding as if she'd just heard tales of famine, massacre, and hopelessness.

"Well, dear," I told her, gratified, "we did what we had to."

Marie's main contribution to these games consists of friendly reports to Little Ricky about the wife and children who await him thirty years into the future. I try to think how the real Little Ricky would have reacted to this information, but he's too long gone. It's very sad. Not sad that I can't remember; sad that I'm concerned about it.

27. Beach vacation

When vacation time comes, some families are beach people and some are mountain people. I spring from a family of automobile people. While little Betsy and her family had been romping on the beach at the Jersey shore, my family was driving between Lincoln's tomb and the Little Bighorn. My dad, avid indoorsman though he was, didn't mind braving the open air for brief walks between our station wagon and a motel, restaurant, or museum. He'd even step out from behind the wheel to stand on the brink of the Grand Canyon or at the foot of Mount Rushmore. So we got to see almost everything you could reach by car.

Maybe this is why I love to travel, but never learned to like the beach. Sure, as a teenager I logged a few hours reddening on the burning sands of Seaside Heights, but if the Gettysburg battlefield had been stocked with nearly naked young women, I'd rather have gone there.

To this day Betsy's parents rent a house on Long Beach Island every July and we spend two weeks with them. I don't like the water, the sand, or the sun, but I do like my in-laws and they like my kids, so I'm always pleased to go.

Besides, Marie and Sally are beach people on their mother's side and I wouldn't want to deny them their heritage. I'll wait until they're older before we introduce them to the ennobling hardships and subtle pleasures of family travel.

Aunt Laura joins us at the beach house and our flocks mingle happily. Uncle Roger shows up when he can. But it's tough for him to get away from Somerville—there's always a chance that a yuppie with a newly extended line of credit will blow into the pet shop and buy a bucket of neon tetras, an aerator strong enough to remove lug-nuts, and a fish tank resembling Lenin's coffin.

Life at the beach house falls into a comfortable routine the first day. The kids wake us up at seven and turn on the TV and it stays on until the last one goes to bed at ten. Sitcoms, game shows, ballgames, and soap operas provide a seamless background to our waking hours. Other years the cousins clustered around the TV like cold bums around a barrel of fire. But for some reason this year they ignore it half the time and draw pictures, fiddle with baseball cards, play Old Maid, or read. It's as if they are a little tired of it, but need to know it's so immediately available that only a shift of attention is needed; the pushing of a button might take too long. Or maybe the sight of a dark, blank, lifeless TV screen scares them, so they must reach out to revive it.

This year there is also a hand-held videogame machine which usually has someone of our party isolated and enslaved.

I alternately play with the kids and read books that have nothing to do with children. Morning and afternoon beach expeditions are launched from our little commune. I attend the morning one and ask to be excused from the other.

The first day I was in the water for five minutes holding Marie when a breaking wave tore her out of my arms, threw her into a churning mix of sand and water, and pushed me powerless down on top of her. If we'd been wearing Fun Badges, they would have turned as purple as fresh bruises by the time we surfaced.

The beach used to make me just uncomfortable, but now it makes me nervous, too. A combination of responsibility and empathy makes me feel like my children are part of me. So where before I had only two feet stepping on hot, scratchy sand and sharp seashell fragments, now I have six. I've got three mouths gulping impure salt-water, and three bodies being burned by the sun, bitten by flies, and buffeted by the surf. I'm getting sand into bodily fissures I never dreamed of having and I can only guess at the discomfort.

When I watch my girls playing anywhere near the water, they seem so fragile and the ocean seems so mighty. Why wouldn't one extra-big wave come along, cascade hugely over the sand and carry them off? To the ocean it would be less than the twitch of a pinky. I know this won't happen, but I *feel* like it might and each wave of any size makes me a little nervous until it has proven its harmless intent by heading back to the deeps without my children.

I have another, more personal problem with the

beach. Other bodybuilders like to show off their physiques, but my building materials have been doughnuts and cheeseburgers. The result is a puffy, pallid creation that does not want to be paraded in public.

Still, the beachly pleasures aren't completely lost on me: Walking along at low tide with Marie collecting shells. Running on the wet sand with Sally, chased by each breaker. On my knees, applying sunscreen to a small, upturned face or rubbing it onto Betsy's brown back, copping opportune, husbandly feels. Just beyond the surf, holding Marie, and jumping to stay above the swells. At night, strolling the beach with Betsy, the kids in bed asleep, in care of their grandparents, also asleep. I can understand what makes the beach people what they are, but I don't think I can ever truly be one of them.

Right on the heels of this year's sandy idyll came the Fourth Guys Weekend, no longer precisely annual, but still important to the guys.

Many years from now I may wonder how I could trade five golden days with my little girls for two days driving to and from North Carolina and three days on a lake torturing live bait with those three mugs. There are lots of reasons. One is that in ten or fifteen years the girls will no longer need me to be totally absorbed in them, so I'd better have something left, besides Betsy, of my old, prefatherhood existence. Another reason was more immediate—a need to be something in addition to a stroller-pushing dad, an obedient husband, and a hump-shouldered copy editor.

Doug joined me in Trenton and we drove all day to rendezvous at Lake Lure with Russ and Tommy who were driving all day up from Florida. It felt good to drive fourteen hours and show up grimy and exhausted. For three days we fished, swam, played low-stakes poker, and caught each other up on our lives and plans while ducks and squirrels rioted around us.

It was relaxing and beneficial and I was glad I went. But I noticed that without Sally and Marie, my visible spectrum of enjoyment was seriously narrowed. It was like being without my eyeglasses. The sensory apparatus for seeing the world as a fresh, exciting place had been left in New Jersey. Those ducks quacking and splashing in the lake below our deck were just ducks to me, but if Marie and Sally were there, they'd have become something special. Their ducklings would be pointed out and exclaimed over, stale bread would be found and thrown to them, and some of the ducks would be given names. Why that squirrel was clattering around on our tin roof and what he had in his mouth would become crucially interesting and important.

This was the flip side of the vulnerability factor mentioned earlier. Sure, their pain is mine, but so is their pleasure. I'd known the two items separately all along, but realizing they are different aspects of the same thing might make next summer's vacation at the beach easier to take.

28. Summer's end

Along this latitude, there's a special end-of-August feeling. Some mornings you wake up chilly and think about football. Outdoors you find a few dead leaves on the ground and notice that the foliage is looking a little tired.

A similar blending of seasons seemed to be happening in the family. Sally could now climb out of her crib and soon we'd either have to string a few courses of concertina wire around the top of her old one or adjust to the change and get her a big-girl bed.

Sally had also developed the ability and inclination to climb onto the toilet. She'd put her foot up on the seat and bring her body up, looking as if she were going to climb right into it, but then she'd turn herself around and sit properly if precariously. She hadn't figured out how to perform up there, despite numerous "potty lessons" from Marie. But Sally was squarely on the road to housebroken respectability and it would only be a matter of weeks before she'd be able to coordinate bodily functions with the assumption of the scoring position.

She was becoming tamed in other areas, too. No longer would Sally eye a disassembled eight-piece puzzle in the blank manner of a New Yorker stepping over a body. Now she'd accept the job and put it together for you with the gung-ho adroitness of a blindfolded Marine reassembling his rifle. Sally was also learning to pick up and stow her toys. She would likewise put her used cup and dishes in the sink. True, she'd heave them in overhand like that same Marine throwing a grenade into a foxhole, but her intent was cooperative even if the result wasn't always constructive.

Marie was growing up, too. Observing the changes, I felt like Henry Fonda, the old fur-trapper in *How the West Was Won*, watching the railroad slash across the plains and knowing an era was ending.

One night Marie couldn't find her special teddy bear. Melly had been missing before, but Marie's reaction had always been near hysteria and no effort was spared until the threadbare creature had been found and tucked into the crook of her arm. This time, however, Marie was nearly indifferent and took the situation as a small challenge to her maturity. She went to bed cheerfully, without even selecting a substitute from the plush and cuddly multitudes that were elbowing each other off her crowded shelves. The next night Melly was back on bedfellow duty, but it saddened me to know the bear's Indian-summer nights were numbered.

There are physical changes, as well. When we'd arrive home late at night with both kids asleep in the backseat, Betsy would see to little Sally and I'd handle Marie. I'd lift her out of the car with a reassuring murmur of "Daddy's got you." Then I'd tenderly carry her up to bed feeling wonderfully fatherly, remembering the warm, lazy, loved feeling I'd had when my own dad used to perform this service for me. But Marie had gotten so long and heavy that, staggering up the stairs under her limp weight, I'd feel like a combat soldier lugging a wounded buddy back from the front line, wanting to shout for a stretcher-bearer.

But the chilliest wind of change swept over me one morning as I lay in bed after a late night in the newsroom. I heard Betsy announce to the girls they could now go upstairs to wake up Daddy. Usually they are eager to wake me up, straining forward like narcotics agents awaiting a search warrant. Once they have the proper authorization, they rush up the stairs chanting, "Da da da Daddy! Da da da Daddy!" They fling open the door and climb into my bed. Snuggling with me, they file reports of early-morning activities, injuries, and injustices and, once I'm up-to-date, they like to worm around awhile in the caves under the blankets, laughing and chattering the whole time. Once when I'd short-circuited these wake-up rites by getting up by myself, Marie had burst into tears of disappointment. But this time I heard her respond casually, "Sally can do it, I'm busy."

As Sally clambered noisily up the stairs I realized it would be only a matter of time before daddy-worship would join the colorful-but-dead religions of the Aztecs and ancient Greeks. "Da da da Daddy!" Sally sang as she swarmed onto the bed to hug my neck, peer into my eyes, and pat my unshaven face.

It struck me hard that no matter how many children we'd have, sooner or later they'd grow up a little and I'd have to be satisfied with just the moderate amount of love that is usually accorded to a moderately lovable person like myself.

29. Starting school

As September and Marie's first day of kindergarten approached, I presented a brave front, not wanting to transmit my anxiety to her.

Nevertheless a number of first-day scenarios unfolded unbidden in my head. In the most painful one, I pictured the teacher addressing the class. "Good morning, children," she says with just the right mixture of kindness and authority. "Can anyone tell the class what day it is?" Whereupon Marie eagerly jumps out of her seat and pulls up her skirt to consult her days-of-the-week underwear. My daydream would end with a wave of derisive laughter rocking the classroom.

Unsophisticated yes, but academically ready. Marie had three years of preschool. Running over the same unchanging curriculum for three years in a row, Marie had studied the alphabet for longer than some clergymen study the Bible. It's inevitable that she would try to write a little.

Often she'd be pretty far off the track, but I wouldn't criticize her work. About a year before, when she'd drawn a backward *S*, I had picked up a pencil and showed her the traditional way. She replied in a tone of stubborn unconcern: "Sorry, Daddy, *this* is the way *I* do it." I pick my fights carefully and I didn't see how I could get into this one and win.

More recently, when Marie made up a menu while playing Restaurant, she wrote "cereal" as "sreailril" and "eggs" as "igz." My wife and I were charmed by her untutored ingenuity and let Marie know it. I'm afraid we're going to leave it to the professionals to burst Marie's bubble by telling her that there's an "a" in "tost" but no "q" in "thank you."

I'm not completely irresponsible, though. For a long time now, I've been steering clear of the traditional fields of academic study, not wanting her to be bored later in class by hearing old stuff. If she were to ask me how a Frenchman would say, "Several rocks have tumbled onto the railroad tracks," she'd be wasting her breath. I'd have to say: "I'm sorry, dear, but your tenth-grade language teacher will tell you that."

Instead I've been trying to teach her things that might not be covered in the classroom. For example, one Sunday in August she learned from me:

1. A dead tree branch will not support the weight that a live branch can.
2. It's the address and *not* the stamp that guides a letter to its destination.

3. When being chased by bears, it's best to run downhill because their short front legs and long hind legs put them off-balance on a down-slope.

Not every day brings such a glittering harvest, but I do my best.

One psychological advantage Marie will have in kindergarten is the fact that our house is visible from the school. Also, the bronze World War I doughboy statue in front of the school has been a character (The Green Man) in stories we've been telling her since she was two. We've deliberately given her the idea that attending The Green Man's school is an extremely lucky and desirable thing.

I tend to cherish rose-colored memories of my own school days. I have managed to revise history to where I was an attractive, athletic, industrious lad— the kind who become millionaires in Horatio Alger stories. But every so often the clouds will blow away and I'll remember that I was almost never fully pre-pared for class and was often nervous and skulking, avoiding eye contact with the teacher, praying that I wouldn't be called on. I usually maintained a grim hope that somehow my homework would do itself before it was due. (I guess the story of "The Shoe-maker and the Elves" had made a deep impression on me.)

Chubby, slow-moving, and clumsy, at least I knew enough to refrain from ballfield clowning. But there was no way I could avoid the shame of being picked last for just about any kind of team.

Once in fifth grade I punched a boy in the face for very little reason except that he was even more unpopular than I was, and I figured that by hitting him I'd boost my own approval ratings.

Was I uniquely unfit and debased or has everyone been unhappily out-of-step at one time or another? I cringe when I think of my little girl entering a place where failure is possible, heartache is likely, and the ignoble deed is commonplace.

Marie may know how to tie her shoes, count to fifty and read a pair of underpants, but she doesn't know how to react to cruelty or rejection. The slightest frustration makes her cry. And to her a mild rebuke is like the stroke of a bullwhip.

Remember the special distress-signal wrist watch that Superman gave Jimmy Olson in the comic books? Whenever Jimmy got into trouble, he'd signal *Zeeeeeeeee* and if Superman were anywhere within the Earth's atmosphere he'd come to the rescue.

I'd like to be able to provide such a service. But maybe that's why Jimmy remained a cub reporter for so long, which in turn may be why kids need to go to school. Besides drinking at the fountain of knowledge, eating paste, and making new friends, kids in school are in line for all those painful-yet-broadening experiences that don't come muscling their way into the hothouse environment of nursery school.

The elementary-school principal sent us a helpful pamphlet entitled "Your Child Entering School." One piece of advice in the booklet seems to be directed at me: "Letting go can be hard, but don't let your doubts or nervousness dampen your child's enthusiasm." I resolved not to, but I wished the local authorities would leave me alone about my doubts and nervousness. They're what keep me going.

30. No good stopping place

Today is Marie's first day of kindergarten. In fact, she's in school as I write this. Luckily Marie is in the afternoon session; a neighbor told us that at the morning session a little boy broke free and bolted for the horizon. He had to be dragged kicking and screaming back across the schoolyard by his mom.

(I hope he's calmed down by now; Marie's probably eating lunch with him as I sit here. In Frenchtown the morning and afternoon kindergarten classes overlap at lunchtime.)

Marie had her outfit selected about two weeks ahead of time—a fetching neon-and-black ensemble of skirt and shirt, featuring bears and kites. She was washed and dressed two hours early. The whole family was going to accompany her. I shaved even though I have the day off. I was about to put on a tie when I realized it isn't *my* first day of school; I only had to look like I have a job. In terms of a "look," that's really all I strive for anymore.

As we all walked across the ballfields, a biplane flew over and I told Marie it was a sign of good luck. She smiled and said, "I don't believe you." I'm lavish with my good-luck omens and Marie is on to me. I took pictures of her holding her pink Minnie Mouse lunchbox, standing beside the familiar Green Man statue on the school lawn. In the lunchbox is a surprise love note from me, which I wrote and put inside at Betsy's suggestion. It's a rebus, its fond hieroglyphics accompanying Marie where I can't.

The kindergarten teacher, Mrs. Doster, stood in the doorway of the old brick school building to greet each child in turn and to pin on a blue construction-paper name-tag. The name-tags had been cut into the shape of birds. Marie kissed each of us and, vibrating with excitement, she entered to receive her name-tag and an education. Sally tried to follow, but Betsy restrained her.

When the last child had entered, all the parents stood around chatting with one another on the front walk until the principal came out, smiled reassuringly, and held up three fingers. "See you at three," he told the group. It was politer than using firehoses to disperse a listless crowd that hadn't made any plans past that moment.

Sally climbed onto Betsy's back and we walked away. I looked back at the old school. Everyone belonging in the school was inside it now and the rest of us were heading home. The front door still gaped open. I'd lived within sight of the school for thirteen years and had been in and out of it a hundred times on newspaper business. Parents had been sending their kids into that school since 1925. Why did I expect it to look different now that it had swallowed up one of mine?

"What are they doing to my baby?" Betsy wondered as Sally rode her slowly across the ballfields toward home. Betsy said it as a joke, but she really meant it, though in a rhetorical way.

I really think Marie will do fine in school, so maybe it's on my own account that I'm sitting at my desk in the bedroom feeling an urge to cry a little. Marie has entered a new phase in her life, a phase in which her daddy will become an increasingly smaller factor. It's healthy and it's proper, but I can't smile about it. Maybe a few more analogies will cheer me up. May I?

I'm thinking about the Scottish sport of curling.

That's the one in which a player, with a mighty heave, skids a forty-pound stone (shaped like a yoyo) out onto the ice hoping it'll come to rest in the middle of a target. Although his teammates aren't allowed to touch the sliding stone, they can make spectacles of themselves rushing around in front of it, feverishly polishing the ice in its path with brooms, hoping to have an ongoing influence on its progress.

From this morning forward, with regard to Marie, Betsy and I will be less and less like the guy who launched the stone and more and more like his frantic partners. We're hoping the throw was good, but we know that the brooms will have to stay in motion for many years to come. In fact, the polishing and sliding goes on and on. Parenthood is more like a long journey along a path than it is like a throw toward an attainable target.

Which is why I make no apologies for the arbitrary selection of Marie's first day of school as the milestone at which to close out this book. There is no obvious stopping place. I'm just reeling off a few yards of material from a thick bolt of cloth. I don't even aim to cut it off and hand it to you. I'd like to just make a chalk-mark here and unroll some more later.

Gotta go; it's almost three o'clock.

Acknowledgments

This book couldn't have been written without the assistance of agent provocateur Russell Galen of the Scott Meredith Literary Agency; my wife and daughters; and my pal Doug Dempsey. And it was awfully nice of Bob Miller of Hyperion to buy the manuscript.

Others who have been helpful include: Russ Stanley, Tom Causey, Kathy Mittler, Joni Scanlon, Charles H. Johnson, Jr., Betty and John Westlake, Nancy O'Reilly, Lynne Gomez, and my brothers.

Some of the material contained in this book originally appeared in regional parenting publications in the United States and Canada.

About the author

Rick Epstein was born in 1951 and graduated from Syracuse University's journalism school in 1973. He is a copyeditor for *The Central New Jersey Home News* in New Brunswick and also writes a monthly column that appears in local parenting publications in the United States and Canada. Mr. Epstein lives in Frenchtown, New Jersey, with his wife, Betsy Westlake, and their daughters.